Parents' Guide to
Raising Kids in a
Changing World

D0167600

Also in the Children's Television Workshop
Family Living Series

Parents' Guide to Raising Kids
Who Love to Learn:
Infant to Grade School

Parents' Guide to Feeding Your Kids Right:
Birth Through Teen Years

Parents' Guide to Understanding Discipline:
Infancy Through Preteen

Parents' Guide to Raising Responsible Kids:
Preschool Through Teen Years

CTW

FAMILY LIVING SERIES ™

Parents' Guide to
Raising Kids in a
Changing World

Preschool Through Teen Years

• • • • • • • • • • • • • •

CHILDREN'S TELEVISION WORKSHOP

Written by Dian G. Smith

Preface by Anna Quindlen

PRENTICE
HALL
PRESS

• • • • • • • • • • • • • •

New York • London • Toronto • Sydney
Tokyo • Singapore

CHILDREN'S TELEVISION WORKSHOP
Chairman, Chief Executive Committee: Joan Ganz Cooney
President—Chief Executive Officer: David V. B. Britt
Publisher: Nina Link

Series Editor: Marge Kennedy
Senior Editor: Sima Bernstein
Writer: Dian G. Smith
Project Editor: Teri Crawford Jones

 PRENTICE HALL PRESS
15 Columbus Circle
New York, NY 10023

Copyright © 1991 by Children's Television Workshop
Line illustrations copyright © 1991 Martha Campbell

Library of Congress Cataloging-in-Publication Data

Smith, Dian G.
    Parents' guide to raising kids in a changing world : preschool
  through teen years / Children's Television Workshop ; written by
  Dian G. Smith ; preface by Anna Quindlen. — 1st ed.
      p.   cm. — (CTW family living series)
  Includes bibliographical references and index.
  ISBN 0-13-650821-9
    1. Parenting—United States. 2. Child rearing—United States.
  3. Family—United States. I. Children's Television Workshop. II.
  Title. III. Title: Raising kids in a changing world. IV. Series.
  Children's Television Workshop family living series.
  HQ755.8.S63 1990
  649'.1—dc20   90-47779
                                        CIP

Designed by Virginia Pope-Boehling

Manufactured in the United States of America

10 9 8 7 6 5 4 3 2 1

First Edition

Acknowledgments

• • • • • •

The staff at the Children's Television Workshop wish to thank Toni Sciarra of Prentice Hall Press for the knowledge and assistance she offered in preparing and editing this series. We also wish to acknowledge the contributions of Anna Quindlen, our preface writer; our advisory panel, whose names and affiliations are listed on pages vii–viii; the writer of this volume, Dian G. Smith; the project editor, Teri Crawford Jones; and researchers Judith Rovenger and ·Nancy DeSa.

Advisory Panel

· · · · · ·

SIDNEY H. ARONSON, Ph.D., is professor of sociology at Brooklyn College and the Graduate Center of the City University of New York. He has taught and lectured on the sociology of marriage and the family for many years and has written extensively on the topic. His articles include "The Ideal Family of American Nostalgia," "Conspicuous Success: The Failure of the Traditional Jewish Family in America," and "Modernization and Socialization: The Problems of Families and Children in a Low-Income Black Community." One of his books analyzes the role of kinship in the structure of the political elite. He is married and has two children.

ANDREW J. CHERLIN, Ph.D., is a professor of sociology at Johns Hopkins University and has published three books and many academic articles on the American family. He has also written articles for the *Washington Post*, the *New York Times*, the *Christian Science Monitor*, *Newsweek*, and the *New Republic*. In 1988 he edited *The Changing American Family and Public Policy* (Urban Institute Press). He is a member of the Panel on Child Care Policy and the Committee on Child Development Research and Public Policy of the National Academy of Sciences and serves as chairman of the Family Section of the American Sociological Association.

ISTAR SCHWAGER, Ph.D., is an educational psychologist, writer, and consultant. She assists in the development of television shows, books, magazines, toys, and other products for parents and children. She is the former director of research of the Children's Television Workshop Magazine Group and, as such, helped launch the *Sesame Street Magazine Parents' Guide*. She currently writes a monthly column for that publication on activities for parents and children.

About the Preface Writer

• • • • • •

ANNA QUINDLEN's column, "Public and Private," appears each week in the *New York Times* and is syndicated in newspapers throughout the country. It is the third column she has written for the paper since she joined it in 1977. From 1981 to 1983 she wrote "About New York," and in 1986 she created "Life in the 30's." A collection of her essays, *Living Out Loud*, was published by Random House. The mother of three children, she was named one of the outstanding mothers in America by the National Mother's Day Committee in 1988. Quindlen's work has also appeared in other national publications, including *McCall's*, *Women's Day*, *Family Circle*, *Ms.*, *Ladies' Home Journal*, *Parade*, as well as in many anthologies.

About the Author

• • • • • •

DIAN G. SMITH is a freelance writer with a master's degree in education from Harvard University. She has written many articles about families and children for national magazines and is the author of four books for young adults and two books for younger children. Her most recent works include *Great American Film Directors* (Julian Messner), *My New Baby and Me* (Scribner's), and *Happy Birthday to Me!* (Scribner's). The mother of three children, Smith was also an author of the Children's Television Workshop Family Living Series book *Parents' Guide to Understanding Discipline.*

Series Introduction

• • • • • •

What do children need to learn about themselves and the world around them if they are to realize their potential? What can parents do to facilitate their children's emotional, physical, and intellectual growth?

For more than a generation, the Children's Television Workshop (CTW), creator of *Sesame Street,* has asked these questions and has conducted extensive research to uncover the answers. We have gathered together some of the best minds in child development, health, and communication. We have studied what experts around the world are doing to nurture this generation. And, most important, we have worked with children and parents to get direct feedback on what it means to be a productive and fulfilled family member in our rapidly changing world. We recognize that there are no simple solutions to the inherent complexities of child rearing and that in most situations there are no single answers that apply to all families. Thus we do not offer a ''how-to'' approach to being a parent. Rather, we present facts where information will help each of you make appropriate decisions, and we offer strategies for finding solutions to the various concerns of individual families.

The development of the CTW Family Living Series is a natural outgrowth of our commitment to share what we have learned with parents and others who care for today's children. It is hoped that the information presented here will make the job of parenting a little easier—and more fun.

Contents

• • • • • •

Preface

• • • • • •

Over the last month I have been asked all of the following questions:

"Mom, can two men get married?"
"How do you get AIDS?"
"Is the ocean polluted?"
"If your parents get divorced, what do you do for a father?"
"Mom, have you ever used drugs?"
"Is that Jonathan's mommy or his baby-sitter?"
"Why did that lady hit her boy?"

This book is called *Raising Kids in a Changing World*, and, like so many other people, that's exactly what I've been doing for seven years. I have three children, two dogs, a husband, a house, a job, a million questions, a lot of confusion, and, in some ways, an entirely different life than my mother had. None of her five children ever asked her any of those questions. She had few divorced friends, no openly gay ones, and none who were mothers and worked outside their homes. AIDS was an unknown acronym, drugs were confined to pharmacies, and baby-sitters came only at night, for special occasions. There was alcohol abuse, and child abuse, and wife abuse, too, in the houses around her, but no one spoke of those things. The bad things were secret then.

Now you can see them on Saturday morning, punctuating the cartoons. "Be smart, don't start," my sons sing along with the public-service announcement, "Drinking hurts." My children have had to be taught not to publicly chastise those who are smoking cigarettes and to wait for a reasonably private moment to ask "What part are the testicles again?" It is a different world from the world in which I grew up.

Lots of people would have us believe that it's an uglier and unhappier world, but I don't believe that's true. And neither does this book. If it has one overriding message, it is that different is just different, not necessarily better or worse. Some kids have moms who go to the office every day, and some have moms who work at home. The ones who have moms who work may go to a day-care center or a baby-sitter, or a baby-sitter may come to them. Some kids have parents who are married to each other, and some have parents who are divorced.

In the past that wasn't true. There was a homogeneity to our family lives that seems soothing in the golden glow of retrospect, particularly when you're trying to keep track of stepparents and visitation schedules and who's picking up the kids at the after-school program. But the price we paid for that homogeneity, that sameness, was a kind of dogmatism. If you weren't the same as everyone else, life was tough.

The price we pay today for diversity is confusion, of course. It is not just confusion about how to answer our kids' questions, but confusion about what we really think of our answers. My kids have lots of the same questions that I had, about sex, about love, about how these relate to the little world inside our house and the big, scary one outside these four walls. The difference is that they've been given permission to ask any and all of those questions. And they've been given to understand that there are no simple answers.

I'm not sure I ever would have asked my mother if two men could marry, but had I done so, her answer would have been short and sure: No. She would have said the same about personal drug use, and she would have been telling the truth. I can't begin to imagine what she would have said about abortion. In fact, looking back, I don't believe I knew there was such a thing until I was in college.

My six-year-old asked about it last week, in the middle of a crowded commuter train. I took a deep breath, and talked. Perhaps not wisely. Perhaps not well. But talk I did, and he listened, and talked, too.

This topic is complicated, and so are our lives. If our education about sex was sketchy, our education about the world was almost nonexistent. I knew more about the Civil War than I did about the history of Vietnam, understood Catholicism as a good Catholic child should but knew almost nothing about Judaism, never for a moment suspected that the planet might run out of clean water or that flipping a bottle in the trash had anything more than a momentary effect. Ask my children about the ocean and they are as likely to talk about industrial pollution and the plight of dolphins caught in tuna nets as about swimming, sailing, or *The Little Mermaid*. Ask them about holidays, and they will mention Christmas and Hannukah. I envy them the breadth of their social education. This doesn't make them any less childlike, but it does make them more completely human.

With this plethora of sensitive issues and seemingly insoluble problems, there are only two possible ways to raise our kids in this changing world. One is to lock them up. That, of course, is out of the question. Or we can talk to them, offer their open minds facts, opinions, and impressions to allow them to keep those minds open and yet shape them, too. I have had to teach my children that there are few questions about life that can be satisfactorily answered with a yes or a no.

Sometimes I've overreacted. Sometimes we all have. Occasionally when I find myself responding to a question about reproduction and going off on some long tangent about the fallopian tubes, I recall that joke about the kid who asked his mother where he came from. Halfway through her tortured recitation of the mechanics, he interrupted. "What I mean," he says, "is Chris says he's from Pittsburgh. Where am I from?"

Raising children has never been easy, and it never will be. A hundred years ago, no mother of a seven-year-old had to explain AIDS or crack or the greenhouse effect. But chances were good that some of her children would never even live to be seven, carried away by ailments for which our kids are early inoculated. Fifty years ago, mothers struggled through the Great Depression, teaching their children to do more with less. My mother may have begun with simple answers. But, while her children were small in the fifties, they came of age in the sixties. Things could not have been worse. One day, sculpted hair, sweater sets, and soda fountains; the next, long hair, no bras, and marijuana. Parents tried to roll with the punches, but it was tough.

The teenagers then, the rebellious, the countercultural, are parents today. We have our work cut out for us. It is difficult sometimes to convince children that they will always be loved if their parents' love for each other has evaporated. It is hard to explain to a child that one of the reasons you go off to work each morning and leave him is because you like to. It takes some doing to let your teenager in on all the pitfalls of drug use when you may have done your own fair share. Teenagers need to know about the consequences and the mechanics of sex while you are hoping with all your heart that they are not having it. It makes you yearn for the days of the easy dictums: Good girls don't. Marriage is forever. All those dictums seem conspicuously unsatisfactory when divorced parents may be trying to have a sex life of their own.

Dictums won't help us now, except for a very simplistic one: Keep talking. We need to talk to our children, to inform, to educate, to inspire, to comfort, perhaps even to enrage. And we need to talk to one another. A considerable difference between the parents of my parents' generation and those of my own is that raising children seemed easier earlier. My mother-in-law, who raised six sons, once told me her standards were different. "We didn't worry about stimulation or careers," she said. "If they weren't bleeding, we assumed they were all right."

It's not that easy anymore. Day care and drugs. Divorce and discipline. Teenage suicide, teenage pregnancy. Two-career families, single-parent families, stepfamilies. There's a lot of work to do. There's a lot of candor and caring required. We need to know our limits, and their limits, too. One wise woman friend said that she was frank and unabashed about explaining sex to her daughter. But when the nine-year-old asked, "How many men have you slept with?" she replied, "There are some things that are none of your business."

"Can I use that?" asked three mothers of younger children gathered round on the playground.

We can use all the help we can get. Some of it is here—the answers to our own questions, and to some of our children's questions, too. Most of them require long and thoughtful answers. A few do not, and some of them have not changed from generation to generation, century to century.

"Do you love me, Mom?"
"Yes."

"Will you help me to grow?"

"Absolutely."

"Do you know all the answers?"

"No. But I will try to find them, for your sake and for my own."

"Can I count on you?"

"Always."

ANNA QUINDLEN

A Few Words About Pronouns

• • • • • •

"The child fell off *his* bike." Or how about "The child fell off *her* bike"? Then again we could say, "The child fell off *his or her* bike." How to deal with pronouns?

If you are a regular reader of *Sesame Street Magazine Parents' Guide,* you know that our policy is to alternate the use of gender-related pronouns. In one paragraph we say *his;* in the following one we use *her.* In a book, that specific policy is not quite as practical—there are just too many paragraphs—but it works in a general way by alternating chapters.

PART I

· · · · · ·

Who We Were

"IF THE MAMA BEAR'S PORRIDGE WAS TOO COLD, WHY DIDN'T SHE STICK IT IN THE MICROWAVE FOR A FEW SECONDS?"

Introduction:
The More Things Change . . .

• • • • • •

The more things change," the French say, "the more they remain the same." These words may be hard to swallow for parents who see around them a world of new and bewildering problems. Listening to the catchwords of today and reading them in the headlines—working mothers, single parents, latchkey children, abused/missing children, teenage mothers, AIDS, crack—parents may yearn for the golden age of their childhood, which they may remember as a simpler, safer, happier time.

Memory, however, often is selective. Adults may choose to remember their parents' anniversary parties, but not their arguments behind closed doors. They may remember the cookies baking in the oven when they got home from school, but not the unapproachable father hidden each night behind his newspaper, his parental duties done for the day once he delivered his paycheck.

Memory also depends on perspective, and certainly parent and child see the same world through different eyes. Ask grandparents if they considered the years when they were raising their families to be the golden age that their grown-up children remember. Most likely *their* "golden age" was the time when they themselves were children! As one mother told her daughter when her first child was born, "You will never sleep soundly through the night again."

For parents today, it is tempting to see abductors around every corner, nitrates in every hot dog, roundworms in

3

every sandbox. But children see a world filled with fascinating things: new people, greasy hot dogs, and inviting sandboxes. And often, in spite of the doom-and-gloom headlines, they are right.

Children also tend to accept the world for what it is, for that is all they know. The problems and dangers they and their friends might face are a familiar, if unpleasant, aspect of their landscape. When parents talk of a changing world, then, it is a world that has changed for *them*, not for their children.

What Has Changed?

There is no denying that changes have taken place since the 1950s, 1960s, and 1970s, when many of today's parents were born or were growing up. And changes will continue to take place. Even isolated communities are not immune. In the movie *The Gods Must Be Crazy*, an empty soda bottle dropped from an airplane disrupts the lives of peaceful bushmen deep in the Kalahari Desert, bringing with it greed and jealousy. In real life, television and newspapers drop society's problems daily into American living rooms—everything from child abuse to rape to drugs. In their own families men, women, and children have had to adjust to working mothers and the possibility, if not the fact, of divorce. Overhearing her parents argue one night, a 10-year-old girl broke in and asked abruptly, ''Are you going to get divorced?''

Dealing with change is difficult, but if parents do it conscientiously—with both their hearts and their minds—children will not suffer and may even benefit. The problems that confront society today may even push them to become better parents. Faced with an untried situation, they cannot get by with the knee-jerk responses they learned from their own parents: "No TV on school nights"; "No sweets during the day"; "Nice girls don't." Their own childhood experiences will not provide pat answers to questions such as "How much time should be spent playing computer games?" and "What about dating or unchaperoned parties for young teens?" With each new question, parents today have to gather all the facts, try to remember what it felt like to be a six-year-old, 10-year-old, 15-year-old, and then think before they speak or act. Parents also may have to rethink their roles as mothers and fathers and perhaps create new models for their children.

Today's parents, of course, are not the only generation that has had to deal with change. During the Great Depression many families faced desperate poverty for the first time. This was obviously not an experience they would have chosen; some of their children had to find jobs to help put food on the table. Yet Glen H. Elder, Jr., a sociologist who studied the lives of children growing up in Oakland, California, during that time, found that their experience of hard times increased their independence, dependability, and maturity in handling money. As adults, they also placed a higher value on marriage, home, and family. If the demands are not overwhelming, Elder concludes in *Children of the Great Depression*, "being needed gives rise to a sense of belonging and place, of being committed to something larger than the self." In a similar way, children with recently separated parents may benefit from the added household responsibilities they usually have to shoulder, so long as these responsibilities are not too great.

Parents today might also benefit from the example of the various supportive family networks that many economically disadvantaged Americans, minorities, and immigrants in this country have created to deal with the problems of poverty and prejudice, and, for some, adjustment to a new way of life. Members of these networks help each other in crises and share job opportunities. They also provide children and adults with an important sense of security and community.

This book will identify and explain some of the changes that have occurred in the world since today's parents were children and provide some guidelines for handling the parenting challenges these changes present. It offers suggestions based on the opinions of experts as well as strategies used by other parents today, in the past, and in other cultures to handle similar problems successfully. The mothers and fathers who tell their stories at the beginnings of chapters were chosen because their lives illustrate some of the issues parents are confronting, as well as some positive responses to them.

The right solution for one family, however, is not necessarily the right solution for all families. Ultimately most parents already have the best tools for raising children in a changing world: good judgment and a set of personal values. These are also the most important legacy they can pass on to their children, the parents of the next generation. Parents who have explored their values and who try to bring knowledge and reason to their decisions can be confident that they are acting in the best interests of their children.

What Has Remained the Same?

Although this book focuses on change, underlying it is a firm belief that two principles have remained the same: The basic developmental needs of children have not changed and will probably never change; and satisfying those needs should be a major goal of all parents. Parents who keep these needs foremost in their mind can best guide their children through a sometimes uncontrollable and unpredictable world.

Thus throughout this book, each suggestion on how to handle new and difficult situations reflects a concern for meeting these basic needs of children:

Love. All children need to know that they are very important to a caring adult—and parents who stay at home have no corner on this market. Even parents who work an overfull day can find countless ways to show their children that they come first. The simple act of leaving a phone number where they can be reached at work or making a regular after-school checkup call or putting a note in a lunchbox or on the refrigerator can remind children that mom or dad is always thinking about them. There is obviously no formula for showing love, but children know, as adults do, when someone is listening and caring, laughing with them and crying with them.

Security. All children need to believe that competent adults will fulfill their physical and emotional needs and protect them from harm. This is perhaps the greatest fear of children after a divorce—What's going to happen to me? Who's going to take care of me? Children do not want to be their parents' confidants, nor should they be asked to bear the burdens of adults' financial and emotional fears. They need to feel safe and to know that their parents' love for them is unchanged.

Continuity. All children need some predictability in their lives. This often comes from following routines and traditions. For busy parents, providing this continuity may mean taking the phone off the hook for an hour every night so that they can put their children to bed uninterrupted; it may mean doing extensive research to find the best available child care; it may mean taking the initiative to create family occasions, even if Thanksgiving dinner consists of take-out turkey and canned yams (and Grandma turning over in her grave). For some divorced parents, it also may mean making it comfortable and easy for a former and detested spouse to remain a part of their children's lives.

Communication. Children need to be able to express their ideas, concerns, and hopes with the confidence that they will be listened to and understood. If the lines of communication are open when children are very young, they are more likely as teenagers to confide in their parents about drugs or sex or terrifying events in the world. But listening takes time, "quality time," not sparing one ear while the news report or the ball game is coming in the other. Many parents create routines to ensure quality time, such as sacrosanct bedtime rituals or family meetings. One mother is grateful years later that she instituted a Sunday family dinner when her children were young. "If it weren't for that," she says, "we might never have seen Justin when he was in high school."

Identity. Children need to feel proud of who they are and where they come from. With this confidence, they can better resist the taunts and temptations of their peers. A sense of identity also affects how children treat others. Before they can reach out with love to people who are different, they must first have a secure sense of who they themselves are.

Belonging. Children need to feel that they are a part of a group that can provide support and guidance. Traditionally this need was supplied by the family, the community, and churches or synagogues. Even if parents are not involved in these institutions the way their own parents may have been, there are still many ways to create networks of support for themselves and their children.

Respect. Finally, all children need to be treated with respect for their age. The information that can be given to a five-year-old about an issue differs from what is appropriate to tell a teenager. Similarly, a five-year-old cannot be expected to behave with the maturity of a teenager. Five-year-olds, for instance, are too young to take care of themselves at home alone after school. By the time they are 12 or 13, however, most children can be responsible for the necessary safety precautions and will not be overwhelmed by fears and loneliness.

With all these thoughts in mind, it is possible to look beyond the negative headlines and find answers to some of the difficult issues parents are facing today.

CHAPTER ONE

•••••

Whatever Happened to Ozzie and Harriet? The Changing Family

Do you think family life in America is in trouble?'' the readers of *Better Homes and Gardens* magazine were asked in the spring of 1988. Of the more than 100,000 who replied, 77 percent said yes. The issues that worried them most were, in descending order:

- Drug and alcohol abuse
- The absence of a religious/spiritual foundation
- Inattentive parents
- Divorce
- Moral decay
- Materialism
- Both parents working

But the ringing of death knells for the family is nothing new; Americans have been hearing them for over a century. ''The family, in its old sense, is disappearing from our land,'' wrote a contributor to the *Boston Quarterly Review* in October 1859, ''and not only our free institutions are threatened but the very existence of our society is endangered.'' In 1912 Anna Garlin Spencer, the first woman ordained as a minister in Rhode Island, wrote, ''There is today a feeling of almost hysterical alarm regarding the present conditions of family life. The demonstrable and large increase of divorces throughout Christendom, the weakening of family ties by reason of changed economic, educational, and social conditions which secure to minor children as well as to wives great freedom of choice and liberty of action, give deep concern to all, and awaken moral terror in many.''

Yet families have a long history of enduring terrible social stresses throughout recorded time. Perhaps the greatest testimony to the family as an institution is its ability to have survived slavery in this country. According to historian Carl N. Degler in *At Odds*, many slaves sought marriage, considering it a lifelong union, even though it might be disrupted when they were sold. While slaves brought together on plantations formed new family networks, separated family members tried and often succeeded in staying in touch with one another. After emancipation, black families aggressively searched for relatives who earlier had been sold or had run away.

In spite of the jeremiads about the dismal state of the family today, marriage and families still seem to be surviving. Recent statistics confirm that most people in the United States marry and that even those who divorce usually remarry. In fact, the proportion of Americans who have reached the age of 50 without marrying is now at its *lowest* point.

The family has not survived by remaining static, however. It has survived by adjusting to social change. Today, in order to raise children successfully, it is helpful to understand the nature of the family as an institution, how it has changed over time, and how it is structured today.

What Are Families For?

Families with children come in many different configurations: two parents and their children, a single parent and children, parents and stepchildren, and extended families of three or more generations. All of them, however, serve the same wide range of functions. Which one or more of the following functions dominate depends on broad social factors (whether the society is rural or urban, for instance) and on events such as economic depression or war.

1. **Reproduction and child rearing.** Families provide for the continuation of the human race. Child rearing also involves fostering children's moral and intellectual development and socializing them to live by the rules of their world. Simple social rules may require parents to toilet train their children by a certain age or teach them to say please and thank you. On a more profound level, parents are responsible for teaching children the values by which they themselves live—the principles of right and wrong, good and bad, which guide their choices and actions. Although social institutions such as schools and churches have taken on some of this teaching, the ultimate responsibility lies with parents.

2. **Economic support and physical protection.** Families provide their young with food, clothing, shelter, and a safe environment in which to live. In the past this role was more critical because society did not provide monetary or institutional support for families that failed. Every member of the family also made an important, tangible contribution to the family's survival. On a colonial farm, for instance, if the children did not do their gardening duties or collect the eggs from the henhouse at the proper time,

13

either everyone had less to eat or someone else had to pick up the slack.

3. **Emotional support.** Providing love and unconditional acceptance has become an increasingly important part of the family's role. During industrialization, as production moved from the home to factories and people began to travel far from their close-knit neighborhoods for work, the family became a comforting haven from the loneliness of an impersonal work world.

How parents choose to fulfill these functions depends partly on their personal values, but they are also greatly influenced by the cultural values that surround them. In their role as parents, Americans traditionally have been confronted by two conflicting cultural values: the importance of the family vs. that of the individual. If the interests of the family come first, then togetherness, stability, loyalty, and mutual responsibility are valued. If the interests of the individual rule, then self-fulfillment and personal growth are primary.

When parents face a choice that is particularly difficult, it is often because these two values have come head to head. One parent, for example, might need to work long hours and weekends in order to satisfy high career ambitions. Another parent might be devoted to a time-consuming hobby. Either of these personal goals obviously conflicts with the desire these parents may also have to spend time with their families.

The resulting choices they will have to make are never easy. They can strive solely for their own self-fulfillment, sacrifice it entirely for their children, or, as many parents do, find a compromise. Whether they can live happily with that compromise may depend upon their general outlook on life, that is, if they tend to see their cup as half empty or half full.

The Premodern Family

Historically, the relative importance of specific functions of the family has varied. Before the United States began to industrialize, most Americans lived on farms or in nearby villages. In these premodern times (before 1800, according to most historians), family and work were completely intertwined. The family supplied its own needs. Family members not only shared the fruits of one another's labors but often worked next to or in sight of each other. Families spent most of their time together because leisure activities, education, health care, and religion often revolved around the family hearth.

In the premodern family, marriages were business as well as personal relationships. They were not prearranged; however, family considerations, such as property and holdings, weighed heavier in the balance than they do today. Parents also had a greater say in their children's choice of spouses, which directly affected the whole family's welfare.

Although everyone in the family did productive work, there was usually a division of labor according to sex: Men planted and plowed in the fields; women stayed closer to home in the orchards, dairies, and kitchens; and children tended to help the same-sex parent. But women's tasks, which included growing, preserving, and preparing foods; weaving; sewing; and generating income by selling the goods they produced, were valued equally as direct contributions to the family's economy.

Because all children in a premodern family had chores and responsibilities, they were valued for their economic contribution and not just as precious objects of love. As future providers, they also represented security for their parents in old age. Childhood and adolescence were not recognized as stages. Childhood was merely the brief period that ended with apprenticeship and the beginning of adult work, usually before puberty. Children started preparing for their adult life at an early age, taking on chores that differed in quantity but not in quality from those of their parents. A seven- or eight-year-old, for instance, might work in the garden, take care of animals, spin wool, dip candles, or prepare meals. A 10- or 11-year-old might be sent for a time to work as an apprentice in another home. And because families were larger, young children could observe in the responsibilities of older siblings working beside them a clear path to adulthood.

Meanwhile, mothers in premodern times did not focus the single-minded attention on their children that came to be expected of them later. They could not; they were simply too busy with other responsibilities. One traveler to eighteenth-century Carolina described the farm woman's duties this way: "The ordinary women take care of Cows, Hogs, and other small Cattle, make Butter and Cheese, spin cotton and flax, help to sow and reap corn, wind silk from the worms, gather Fruit and look after the House." In addition, during the eighteenth century and well into the nineteenth, women made most of the clothing their families wore.

In Early American families, the father was the parent expected to be most involved in many aspects of child rearing: instilling moral and religious values, teaching reading and writing, planning the children's marriages. Men's superior reasoning abilities, so it was believed, better equipped them for this role and made them better models of good character and right behavior. Children were thought to have come into the world marked by sin, driven by powerful passions, and possessed of a will that must be broken. Since a mother, it was feared, might spoil her child by being too indulgent, her role in child rearing was limited. When there was a marital separation, the common law gave custody to the father.

These are not the aspects of the premodern period (and even more recent periods) that most people today yearn for when they look back nostalgically at family life in the past. Perhaps the most appealing aspect of that life to modern Americans is the idea of an extended family living happily together: the image of Grandma rocking Baby in his cradle so that Mom can help arthritic Uncle Ned to the table for a Sunday dinner for 20.

But never, as far back as records go, was it common for three or more generations of one family, including married brothers and sisters with their children, to live together (happily or unhappily) in one household. Throughout Europe as long ago as the Middle Ages, the great majority of people resided in nuclear families. Life expectancy then was much shorter, and rarely were many members of two or more generations even alive at one time. The nuclear family, consisting of husband, wife, and their children, has always been the basic family unit in Western life.

Many historians, in fact, consider the involvement of grandparents in the family to be a modern phenomenon—the result of improved medical care and longer life expectancy. Today people aged 60 and older make up about 15 percent of the population. In early New England communities they comprised about 4 to 7 percent. Those grandparents, however, did live nearby, and often families enjoyed regular contact with a network of relatives who settled in the same village or neighborhood.

Some family members remained in a community from birth until death. Brothers, sisters, cousins, and in-laws met in the village square or at church on Sunday—much more frequently than is usual today. Growing up surrounded by relatives gave children a sense of identity and the security of being part of a family and community. Even the large number of Americans who moved (the rate was nearly as high in the 1800s as it is today) tended to settle in small communities, where neighbors felt responsible for each other and became involved in each other's affairs.

Premodern households themselves also served a more public role than they do today, often containing strangers along with the nuclear family—boarders, apprentices, and servants. Delinquent youths, orphans, and abandoned elderly people might also be placed with families. Later, social institutions took over these functions, communities grew and became less neighborly, and families became more private.

Factories and Cities

By the time of industrialization in the mid- to late 1800s, important changes had occurred in American family life. The shift from independent farming to working for wages altered the relations between husband and wife, parents and children, and the family and society. The family structure that appeared is the one that survives today.

Work and home were separated for the first time, so that men and women occupied two different spheres. Men took on the central role of breadwinner. And because their new schedules required them to be away from their wives and children for many hours of the day, fathers' involvement in child rearing became part-time and distant, much as it often is today. The law of child custody reflected this change, so that by the end of the nineteenth century, women were generally given custody in marital separations.

Men's status as providers rose, but they lost their image of moral superiority in the home. Toiling in the dangerous outside world, they were suspect of being compromised in unsavory ways on the road to success. They needed to return home to shake the soot from their garments. The family and home were, thus, idealized as a private retreat from a harsh, cold, and possibly sinful world.

As the father's role in child rearing waned, the mother's grew. So did her aura of moral purity, which now was seen to qualify her for motherhood. She became solely a homemaker, a domestic role in which she was sometimes glorified. The assumption that the full-time job of women was to care for the well-being of home and children became part of the ideology of American family life in the mid-nineteenth century for the first time.

Historians argue whether the industrial-age woman was better or worse off than the premodern woman. Although her role as economic equal was lost and she was now confined to the home, this "new woman" had a certain amount of power within the family as child rearer and moral guide of both children and husband. And she was not idle. Many such women spent long, hard hours managing their homes and children in a world where water still had to be carried, laundry was done by hand, and food was cooked on a wood-burning stove.

Historian Carl N. Degler argues that the nineteenth-century powerful father and subordinate mother are myths. In many cases, women were the confidantes and companions of their husbands in a new way, and marriages were based much more on romance, affection, and respect. Unlike the eighteenth-century husband, who might address his wife in a letter as "Dear child," nineteenth-century husbands in their correspondence readily admitted dependence on their wives for friendship, sympathy, and sometimes advice.

The birthrate also began to decline in the early nineteenth century. In 1800 the average white family had seven children; in 1900 the average had dropped to three or four.

Degler suggests that this was women's choice, for it clearly eased the burden on those who bore and raised those children. It also changed the nature of marriage and parenthood. Less time spent on raising large numbers of children gave marriage a separate importance of its own.

The view of childhood, too, changed in the nineteenth century. Children began to be seen as innocents, recently arrived from heaven and close to God. In "Ode: Intimations of Immortality from Recollections of Early Childhood" (1807), the Romantic poet William Wordsworth addressed the child as "Mighty prophet! Seer blest!" Children, according to this new view, no longer needed to be tamed, but to be nurtured and protected from the corruptions of the world. For the first time childhood was recognized as a distinct and valuable stage. Birthdays began to be celebrated and the use of corporal punishment as a form of discipline greatly declined.

Children in the middle class, like their mothers, were separated from the world of work in order to lengthen this special stage. Those in urban areas did not start to work until their late teens and no longer contributed to the home economy. In *Pricing the Priceless Child*, sociologist Viviana A. Zelizer describes the emergence in 1870 of "the economically worthless but emotionally priceless child." Although the change in attitude took longer to reach the working class, child labor laws and compulsory education enforced it by the 1930s.

Another characteristic of the mid- to late nineteenth century was the split between public and private life. Social institutions (public schools, churches, hospitals, asylums, prisons, and reformatories) gradually assumed some of the family's functions of education and care. The home became a private family residence focused on child care and child rearing. The mother, father, and children became more closely involved with one another, and their ties with their relatives as well as with the larger society weakened. The nuclear family became more isolated physically, too, when the suburbs had their first boom of popularity in the late nineteenth century. Mom and dad might now live many miles away from grandma and grandpa.

Twentieth-Century Family Life

By the early decades of this century, the ideal American family was thought to be a father who was the breadwinner, a mother who was a full-time homemaker, and their natural children, all living together in the same house. Today that image still tends to prevail. Yet in 1985 married couples with children under 18 in which the husband was the sole wage earner made up less than 30 percent of families and less than 10 percent of the population as a whole. What happened?

The present high rate of divorce is a major phenomenon of this century. Before the medical advances of the beginning of the twentieth century, mothers and fathers often died while their children were still young. As late as 1940, more than twice as many children lost a parent from death as from divorce. In most families today, both parents live to see their children to adulthood. And marriages are much more often ended by divorce than by death.

There was a slow, steady increase in the annual rate of divorce through the end of World War II. Then the trend fluctuated. From 1950 to 1962 the divorce rate was lower than had been expected. Then it doubled between 1965 and 1985, peaking between 1979 and 1981. Before 1960 about one in nine children had experienced parental divorce; by 1980 it was one in three. Since then the rate has leveled off, but the United States Census Bureau predicts that in the

1990s, 40 percent of children will see their parents divorce.

As divorce increased, so did the number of families headed by women. Single-parent homes jumped from 11 percent of families with children in 1975 to 23 percent in 1988. Early in the century it was common for divorcing parents to send their children to live with relatives or for a divorced mother to move in with her parents. Today most single parents (usually mothers) live alone with their children. And when fathers leave, they not only remove a male figure from the household but also remove their income. Divorced women generally suffer a greater financial decline than do their former husbands, and only a minority of divorced fathers continue to provide financial support for their children.

The nature of remarriage has changed, too. Now three out of every four divorced women and five out of every six divorced men remarry. One in every four children is a stepchild. As divorce has replaced death as the primary cause of nuclear-family breakups, however, a new element has been added to the stepfamily. Now the other natural parent is still alive, although living in a different household. Remarriages can create complex kinship patterns and intimate bonds sometimes with nonblood relatives—the stepfather's parents, for instance, or his children from a previous marriage. A child's relationships may bridge several households, and a seemingly simple assignment for a second grader to draw a picture of her "family" may take on a mind-boggling complexity.

Although the issues of divorce and remarriage now touch many families, society has not yet established norms for appropriate behavior within these new contexts. Even the question of what name to use for a stepparent has not been resolved; solutions range from first names to "Daddy John" and "Auntie Mom." It may be in part because of this uncertainty that the divorce rate for remarried couples is consistently, though only slightly, higher than for first marriages.

One explanation historians give for the rise in divorce in this century is the greater importance modern couples put on the marital relationship. In the second half of the twentieth century, the focus of the family has shifted from children to spouses. Parents today can expect to spend 25 years together without children and about 40 years without small children. As expectations of personal fulfillment in marriage rise, the possibility of failure increases. Today's unhappy couples are more likely to divorce and perhaps try again.

It is, in part, because of another twentieth-century phenomenon—the increase in work opportunities for women and their resulting economic independence—that divorce has become an option for those caught in unhappy marriages. This trend, then, has led to a rise in the number of working mothers of young children.

From the nineteenth century until World War II, almost all women in the work force were single. In 1940 fewer than 12 percent of married white women worked outside the home and most of them had grown children. Among black women the figure was higher, about 25 percent, largely because they had to supplement the low incomes of their husbands and fathers.

In recent decades this pattern has changed sharply. In 1940 fewer than 10 percent of women with children under six were in the work force; in 1950 it was 12 percent; in 1975 36.6 percent; and in 1988 more than 57 percent. Women were drawn into the job market during World War II by feelings of patriotism and the availability of jobs and higher wages due to the shortage of male workers. Most women returned to the home when their soldiers came marching back to resume the role of breadwinner. Some women kept their jobs, however, and their numbers increased in the 1960s, when prosperity once again expanded work opportunities for them.

Yet even today, in two-job families, home duties are usually viewed as women's work, although children and fathers may help. Despite talk of the "modern man" and the "new father," working women still spend more time performing housekeeping and family-related chores than do their husbands. And despite their progress up the corporate ladder, many married women continue to view their work as secondary, a supplement to their husbands' incomes.

Beyond the long-term historical trends, however, each of the last four decades has had a special impact on attitudes toward women's work and other aspects of family life today.

The 1950s: Father Knew Best

Even those who are too young to have seen the original broadcasts of "The Adventures of Ozzie & Harriet" (on prime-time television between 1952 and 1966) or "Father Knows Best" (on the air from 1954 to 1963) can conjure up the image of the TV family of the 1950s: a middle-class family living in a suburban house filled with all the modern conveniences; a father with a good job; a mother in the kitchen wearing a shirtwaist dress and pearls (at 8 A.M.!); and two or three happy children, the oldest of whom is wheedling his father into giving him the keys to the station wagon.

This television fairy tale was in many respects true. In the 1950s nearly everyone married, and nearly every married couple who could do so had children. The rate of childbearing was unusually high by twentieth-century standards (1957 was the peak of the baby boom), and the rate of divorce was unusually low. During this decade women married earlier than they did in the 20 years before or after. More married women had two or more children than their mothers had had or their children now have.

In *Marriage, Divorce, Remarriage,* sociologist Andrew J. Cherlin, Ph.D., examines some of the reasons for this decade-long blip in demographic statistics. Some observers claim that after the war a general shift in attitudes placed increased value on marriage and children. Exhausted by the war and the economic collapse that preceded it and able to take advantage of an economic boom, young adults may have wanted to retreat into their private lives to heal.

Others believe that the trauma of the Great Depression affected the children and adolescents of the 1920s and 1930s (who became the parents of the 1950s), intensifying their desire for marriage and children. These men and women saw their fathers unemployed or marginally employed and their family life disrupted. In families that were hit hard, young boys often were forced to get jobs and become independent, and girls bore a heavy share of household work. As young adults, they may have wanted to get married quickly and enjoy the comfortable family life they had missed. Postwar prosperity and the high demand for young workers made this possible. Because many such young people had grown up in tightened circumstances, they also may have placed a lower value on material goods and thus had a lower expectation of lifestyle. As adults, they reasoned, they could have a relatively large family and still satisfy their modest desire for possessions with a single income.

Probably, Dr. Cherlin writes, both of these factors—changed social attitudes and the childhood and young adult experiences of fifties parents—contributed to the growth of Ozzie-and-Harriet households, which marked this demographically peculiar decade in American history and interrupted the trends toward later first marriages, declining birth rates, and high divorce rates, which we see today. ''Had the 1940s and 1950s not happpened,'' one study concluded, ''today's young adults would appear to be behaving normally.''

The 1960s and 1970s

In the 1960s the demographic zig took its zag. It was a time of optimism and of social upheaval—the birth of the civil rights and antiwar movements, the rebirth of the women's movement, and the arrival of the sexual revolution. People proclaimed the right to be themselves, to ''do their own thing.'' And unlike earlier parents, those who became fathers and mothers in this generation had high expectations and a taste for material things.

One zag was the return to a skyrocketing divorce rate, which affected long-term marriages as well, and the resulting rise in the number of single-parent families. No longer was divorce seen as a shameful sign of failure. To many, divorce meant liberation and proof of positive change.

During the 1970s the marriage rate fell and the birthrate hit an all-time low. More and more men and women were delaying marriage, possibly due in part to the better methods of contraception that became available during this period. Another cause of these declines may have been a demographic squeeze. Women have long tended to marry men a few years older. However, because of the rising birthrate in the 1950s and 1960s, women of marriageable age in the 1970s outnumbered men born earlier. The Vietnam War also took a high toll of young men. The number of unmarried couples living together more than tripled between 1970 and 1983. Cohabitation did not replace marriage, but it became, in many circles, an accepted stage of courtship.

Some scholars believe that the most important factor in these demographic changes was the great increase in young women working outside the home in the 1960s and 1970s. With an independent means of support, these women had the freedom to delay marriage or to end it.

By the late 1970s, the optimistic mood of the 1960s had changed, partly because the social and economic conditions that had fueled it also had changed. For the first time in history, Americans had to face the possibility that their children might not lead better lives than theirs. There also was an atmosphere of deflated hope: John F. Kennedy, Robert F. Kennedy, and Martin Luther King, Jr., had been assassinated. American society had not been transformed as those who had challenged it had hoped and expected. The war in Vietnam and the scandal of Watergate had convinced many people that America was not all-powerful and its leaders not always honorable.

The 1980s—and Beyond

Although the rates of marriage, divorce, and childbirth seemed to stablize in the 1980s, they still bode a world of diverse family forms for parents and children in the future: two-parent families, single-parent families, stepfamilies, blended families, one-wage-earner and two-wage-earner families. Nearly half of recent marriages are projected to end in divorce, more and more marriages that break up today include children, and 23 percent of families are headed by single parents. Researchers estimate that the majority of all children alive today will probably witness divorce in their lives—either in their parents' marriage or in their own. More than half of the children born in 1987 will spend at least one year living in a single-parent household before the age of 18.

In the 1980s the largest increase in the work force came from mothers of infants. Working mothers promise to keep pushing at the boundaries of the family until it accommodates them, thus changing the experience of childhood and of parenthood. The family of the future, for instance, without its resident housewife and mother, may expect more help from its children at home. Men may be forced to embrace an expanded definition of their roles as husbands and fathers. Nonrelated caregivers will become increasingly important partners in child rearing. In addition, industry will be pressed for more flexible working conditions and the government will be pressed for more and better day care.

Today's children will have to adjust to a much greater number of family settings in their lives than did their parents. Writing in *The Futurist* magazine (June 1983), sociologists Andrew J. Cherlin, Ph.D., and Frank F. Furstenberg, Jr., Ph.D., predicted this life history for a substantial number of the children born in the 1980s: "[They will] live with both parents for several years, live with their mothers after their parents divorce, live with their mothers and stepfathers, live alone for a time in their early twenties, live with someone of the opposite sex without marrying, get married, get divorced, live alone again, get remarried, and end up living alone once more following the death of their spouses." How well these children survive and thrive will depend largely on how well their parents prepare them for change by giving them basic values and an understanding of the world.

The 1980s, like the decades that preceded it, had its own emotional aura. It started with a strong antifamily ring, but some claimed it was ushered out by the "New Traditionalist"—"the most powerful social movement since the sixties," according to a 1989 ad in *Good Housekeeping* magazine based on material from Yankelovich Clancy Shulman, a national polling firm. ''My fundamental values,'' the imaginary New Traditionalist reports, ''haven't changed from those that my mother taught us as children.'' The spirit of new traditionalism, according to reporter Stephen Holden in the *New York Times* (August 13, 1989), ''is gently puritanical and politically ambivalent and eager to preserve liberal attitudes—but not liberal activism—in a conservative climate.''

Whether or not parents see themselves as part of this ''movement,'' it does invite them to step outside the whirl of change and ask themselves, What hasn't changed? What values were we taught and what still holds true for our lives today? What values are we teaching our children—and how?

CHAPTER TWO

• • • • • •

Parenting Today: Old Values in a New World

My mother and my father taught me many of the same values I am trying to teach my children. My parents were strict in a benevolent way. I don't remember being punished, and my sisters and I were never hit. But they somehow instilled values in us—probably by example.

Although my mother was at home with us, she was very active and creative. I had a sense of her as a person who was important in the community. She taught us to finish what we started and to take pride in what we did. My mother was a role model for me as a doer. Although our lives are different, somehow the underlying themes are the same. My children see me being responsible by getting up every morning and going to work. They've gone with me to my job and have seen what I do.

My father worked very hard. We had nice things and he built a good life. He taught us that you had to work to get something, and you appreciated the value of it and took care of it. I want my children to have fine things, but I want them to know the worth of those things.

My mother also taught us not to hurt other children or to be mean to people. If we were having a birthday party, she always wanted us to invite everybody. I've done that with my children, too. There are times when I've said, ''You may not like Sally or Joe, but you don't have to be mean. If the rest of the class is being mean to somebody, you don't have to join in.'' That's a value I think is important.

My children see me interacting with other people, in business settings and with my friends. They see that I have to be concerned about other people's feelings and that you have to be able to get along with all different kinds of people.

My family always had dinner together. It was a time when we all talked about what we'd done that day. Maybe just their interest in our lives was a way that my parents taught us values. Sometimes I'm not home for dinner, but we do something almost every night that solves the same problem in a different way. The children and I get into my bed and talk for a few minutes. That's when they tell me the things I would have told my mother and father at the dinner table in the more traditional setting.

My family also had religious values. We went to church every Sunday. As a single parent, with everything else I have to do to get through the week, going to church has been one of the things I find difficult to do. But I do think my children have a sense of religion. My daughter goes to a Catholic school, and my son is going to take his first Communion next year. I am pursuing it with my children because a religion teaches you values, and I think it's important for them to have them.

Although I am divorced, I don't think my values about relationships or what relationships should be are any different from my parents' values. I am a firm believer in people being loyal. But I don't think people should stay in unhappy relationships, which perhaps my parents' generation did.

I got the idea from my parents that you are ultimately accountable for your actions. I've come right out and told my daughter when I've done something wrong. And I've told her that when you do something wrong, you pay a price for it at some point in time. My expression to her is: Payback is a bitch.

I talk much more frankly with my kids than my parents did. When I grew up, sex wasn't discussed openly and we didn't have the problem of AIDS. But now the times are different. Everything has a sexual connotation. I wish I could have had open conversations with my parents, and that's why I have them with my children.

Although the world is different now, I think the worst problem parents still face, no matter what the issue, is peer pressure. I ran with a fast crowd when I was young, but there were things that I just didn't do. I absolutely know I didn't do them because of my parents. My parents were never dictators. Although they set limits, it wasn't for the sake of limits. My mother used to say, "Always give children a way out. If you back them into a corner, the only way they can come out is at you." So my mother would say to us, "Don't get into a car with somebody who's been drinking. It's a dangerous thing to do. Call us from wherever you are, even if it's someplace you're not supposed to be." And somehow my parents created a mutual respect. I didn't want to get drunk and maybe get arrested because I would disappoint them.

I would like to think that my children respect my feelings about things. This doesn't mean they won't test the waters, like sneaking with their friends to a movie that I don't want them to see. But I have an intuitive sense that there are some things they are not going to do because of the way I am with them, because we talk about things, perhaps because I am stern, because I have given them a sense of what is right and wrong, as my parents gave me.

—A MOTHER

The woman speaking grew up in a small town, in what she calls "a traditional setting." Her father was the breadwinner. Her mother never held a paying job. Her parents were married till their deaths. Her own adult life is very different from theirs. She is the mother of a 13-year-old and a nine-year-old. She has been divorced (and single) for six years. She lives in a big city and works full-time. Yet she is teaching her children many of the same values she was taught to guide them through life. Her way, of course, would not suit everyone, but the message of her story does: Parents, even in a changing world, do not have to reinvent the wheel. Cloth diapers may go in and out of style, but as psychologist William Damon, Ph.D., author of *The Moral Child*, writes, ''the core unquestioned values of our culture are never outdated.'' For most people, these include such moral virtues as honesty, kindness, a sense of responsibility, and a sense of fairness.

Like the woman quoted above and her mother and father, all parents transmit messages to their children about how to behave toward others and live in the world by the manner in which they play the role of parent in general and of mother or father in particular. They may also choose to emphasize certain personal, social, political, and religious values. Some of these choices may seem clear; others are far more complicated. For parents caught in this dilemma, it should be helpful to explore the range of options for families today.

Choosing Between Me and We

The most basic choice men and women make as parents is how much of themselves to invest in their family life. Building a feeling of togetherness in a family requires time, effort, and thought, which otherwise could be devoted to individualistic pursuits. Even with the greatest investment, parents may never create the ''ideal'' American family that Norman Rockwell portrayed on canvas, happily gathered each night for a home-cooked meal. But children who see their parents choose family over self— giving up golf dates and dinner parties to attend class plays, Little League games, and recitals—learn by example that the family is highly valued and is something on which they can depend.

Finding the time to foster family bonds is often difficult. Many parents and children today are tied to conflicting schedules dictated by work, school, after-school jobs and activities, and community responsibilities. One woman was distressed to hear her son explain to his teacher on the telephone that his mother couldn't help him with his math homework because she was going to her class and that his father couldn't help "because he gets home too late."

The harried nature of people's lives is nothing new. As long ago as 1840, the historian Alexis de Tocqueville wrote of the American that he "is always in a hurry." At the turn of the century the average work week was six days long, with 10-hour days. What *is* new is that children are often separated from both parents for much of that time.

The situation is not hopeless. Families develop innumerable imaginative schemes for being together, turning chore time and driving time, for instance, into enjoyable personal times. Some families encourage their teenagers to bring their friends home rather than go elsewhere, by providing a relatively private space and a liberal attitude toward messes. Some families save Sundays or every other weekend for activities together. Some families take yearly vacations, creating memories that last a lifetime (be they the sound and smell of an ocean beach at sunset or the time the car overheated and Dad poured pink lemonade onto the engine to cool it). And studies have shown that simply by reading to their children regularly parents draw their families closer.

Family traditions also are a strong glue. They may re-

volve around religious and national holidays, birthdays, an-
niversaries, or anything at all (testing the first snow together
with sleds and sharing hot cider afterward, raking leaves in
the fall and jumping on the stacks, or shopping for new
school supplies in September). Documents, such as photo-
graph albums and videotapes, also help to create a family
history and identity. Some families have regular family
meetings, in which parents and children discuss issues and
problems (from allowances to sibling rivalry) and try to
share opinions and resolve conflicts together so that tensions will not build up over time.

And parents need not give up on the family meal. It does
not have to be every night and it need not be home-cooked,
but it is still an invaluable focus for family life. One family,
for instance, meets at a nearby fast-food restaurant after the
boys' soccer games on Wednesday nights. Another family
has special Sunday breakfasts together. Especially when
children become teenagers and are on their own much of
each day, an established routine of sitting down with the
family at least once a week can be a restful time-out for
them and a useful check for their parents.

Because time always seems scarce, it is easy for even con-
scientious parents to shortchange their families without re-
alizing it. Some parents find it helpful to make a list
occasionally of the activities that fill their days and to order
them by priority, eliminating those that have eaten away at
family time. This is also an activity children can do along
with parents. It will help them to understand that togetherness is a value that necessitates changes in their parents'
lives as well as in their own.

Parenting Styles

Parenting style, or the way in which parents raise their children, also transmits parental values. Some parents emphasize achievement, or self-denial, or personal growth, and their expectations of their children's behavior will reflect this.

Based on a 20-year study, sociologist Diana Baumrind, Ph.D., of the University of California at Berkeley identified three discipline styles that cover the range of what most American parents use. They differ primarily in their balance of power between parents and children. At one end of the spectrum are authoritarian families, in which the parents have most of the power and dictate their children's behavior. At the other end are permissive families, in which the children have most of the power and are allowed to direct their own behavior and sometimes their parents' behavior as well. Somewhere in the middle are authoritative families, in which the ultimate power is still the parents', but they explain their reasons and consider their children's arguments.

Most of the men and women who are parents today were raised in an authoritarian style, though some were raised permissively. Very few experienced the authoritative style, which combines the communicativeness and warmth of permissive parenting with a demand for mature behavior. Behind it is the belief that all families need rules and routines, and that children are more likely to obey these rules and routines if they have a say in what they are. Parents retain the right, however, to deem certain issues nonnegotiable. These might include curfews for teenagers, bedtimes for younger children, the necessity to attend school and work hard, or the need to respect their own property and that of others.

Ideally, this style of child rearing encourages communication and respect within the family and helps children to develop both self-discipline and self-esteem. Dr. Baumrind found that children raised authoritatively were likely to be socially responsible and competent. Likewise, in a study of adolescents, sociologist Glen H. Elder, Jr., found that the most self-confident and independent teens were those who were raised in this more democratic manner. These children also admired and emulated their parents and accepted their moral standards. "Authoritative adult-child relations," according to psychologist William Damon, "in which firm demands are made of the children while at the same time there is clear communication between adult and child about the nature and justifications of these demands, yield the most positive results for children's moral judgment and conduct."

Damon gives a number of explanations for this. Authoritative parents, he writes, support children's natural empathy by pointing out when they are acting in ways that might hurt others. They communicate the value of obeying legitimate authority, and by enforcing their demands, they demonstrate their commitment to them. They act directly and honestly, and their consistent use of authority makes them attractive role models. Damon also points out that authoritative parents make demands on their children that are challenging but not unrealistic.

Although many experts today seem to advocate the authoritative parenting style, many would probably also agree that the best system for a family is the one with which both parents feel most comfortable. And this may well be more permissive or more authoritarian than a theoretical model. Parents who are thoughtful child rearers, however, can take advantage of the strengths and compensate for the shortcomings of whichever approach or combination of approaches they choose.

Permissive parents, for instance, who encourage their children to express their feelings and rarely confront them about any bad effects of their actions, may have to make certain distinctions clear (for instance, that having permission to say they are angry is not the same as having permission to hit their mother or brother). In the absence of clear-cut rules, they may also have to be careful not to spend so much time begging, cajoling, nagging, and wishing aloud that their children's behavior would change than they create the very tension they may be trying to avoid.

In more authoritarian families, parents need to be careful to ensure that their children are not obeying rules only out of fear of being punished. Such behavior fails to foster self-control in the absence of rules. Children in these families will need some opportunities to make their own decisions. To temper the strict discipline, authoritarian parents should give their children a great deal of love and help them understand that they have only their children's best interests at heart. One mother who has managed this successfully received a Mother's Day card that her eight-year-old son made in school, in which he wrote: "My mother likes me a lot when I'm good because she's strict, but in a nice way. The best thing about my mother is how much she loves me."

Mothering

A generation ago there was more consensus about proper methods of child rearing, and the roles of men and women in this endeavor were clearly defined. The word *parenting* did not exist; the emphasis was on mothering. The wisdom of the time stressed the importance of a child's early years and gave mothers alone the critical role of fulfilling the infant's needs. Sigmund Freud, who introduced the concepts of psychoanalysis, believed that an infant's relationship with his mother affected his personality development and all future relationships. Later another influential psychoanalyst, John Bowlby, M.D., who studied orphaned children living in institutions after World War II, proclaimed the importance of the child's attachment to the mother and the harm caused by "maternal deprivation." Women of that era were thus brought up to believe that young children could best be cared for only by their mothers and that any separation might permanently scar them.

Yet the glorified role of mother makes unrealistic and troubling demands on women. As the poet Adrienne Rich wrote in her nonfiction study *Of Woman Born*, "I was haunted by the stereotype of the mother whose love is 'unconditional' and by the visual and literary images of motherhood as a single-minded identity."

Mothers today still cannot win. Tongues cluck whichever way they turn, even though most people now know that a child's future is not determined by a single incident in infancy but by a pattern of treatment, and that fathers, too, can be able caregivers. "Possibly the only arrangement that would generally be approved as ideal," Beppie Harrison, a mother of four, writes in *The Shock of Motherhood*, "would be one in which a mother of young children had a well-paid, part-time job in the area of her greatest personal interest, located conveniently within five minutes of home, with flexible hours that enable her to be at home when the children need her or not to come in at all if they are sick, with weekends and school vacations off."

Few women have this arrangement, and even those who can choose whether or not to work while their children are young still have to face disapproval whatever choice they make. In addition, many women with full-time jobs outside the home have few role models from their mothers' generation to follow, while those who stay home lack the social supports their mothers had.

Today's mothers have been promised a rosy future of child rearing and homemaking equally shared by both parents, but some cultural traditions and social institutions change slowly, while changes may come too quickly in others. Society's overall approval of professional working women, for instance, has increased greatly in the past 20 years, yet most of the jobs these women hold are still designed for workers with wives at home. And the idea that work in the home is women's responsibility has changed little. Even in households with full-time working mothers and husbands who claim to be committed to equality, women still do much more of the child care and housework.

Since "having it all" has proved to be an impossible combination of conflicting values, mothers today need to weigh carefully the choices they inevitably will make and then settle for less than perfection in every arena. The daughters of spick-and-span moms will have to learn to laugh when they overhear their children say as a child does in one of Beverly Cleary's children's books, "My mother is a terrible housekeeper. . . . She says she doesn't need neatness. . . . She says she has more important things to do than try to keep a house full of boys neat. She says it's a losing battle."

Fathering

Men today have been put in a double bind also, expected to be both nurturing fathers and ambitious, successful breadwinners. The great interest in fathers as active participants in child rearing is new, resulting in part from the women's movement and the growing number of mothersin the work force. Only a generation ago it was assumed not only that fathers were less important to the developing infant but also that they were by nature incapable of child rearing.

The first postfeminist studies of fathers, beginning in the early 1970s, mainly compared men with women in their interactions with children. Psychologist Ross D. Parke, Ph.D., author of *Fathers*, and others found that men were able to perform many of the child-rearing functions traditionally done by women. Men also have a natural capacity for nurturing, according to Dr. Parke. During the first year, infants attach to their fathers as well as to their mothers. Fathers can be just as sensitive and responsive to infants' signals and cries, though they may differ in their responses (fathers tend to be more physical in their play and mothers more verbal).

Today most men are more willing than their fathers were to share the parenting role with women. In the past, according to some studies, fathers did only about 20 percent of the family work; today they do about 30 percent. Men also are demanding to play a greater role in their children's lives after divorce.

Some social changes that occurred in response to working mothers' needs are affecting working fathers, too. Paternity leaves and flexible work hours allow some men to spend more time with their children. Generally, however, businesses do not yet accept, much less reward, the notion of men taking time off for child care or putting their families above their careers. As working mothers have long known, employers prefer single-minded careerists, and co-workers who are single or childless often consider special privileges for parents unfair.

For an ambitious man, as for an ambitious woman, being

a parent requires making difficult choices. Most of today's women with children were socialized to be mothers, encouraged to play with dolls or care for younger brothers and sisters; few men were trained to be fathers. They have few role models among their own fathers and they have received little education for this role.

In many ways, the "new father" is no more real than the "supermom." This role, too, involves an impossible conflict of values. The types of real fathers today cover the spectrum from men who are as little involved with their children as were their own fathers to a few men who have reversed parenting roles with their wives. Men's roles are in transition, and each father has to choose his own place.

In one of his columns for *Newsweek* magazine (April 3, 1989), journalist Robert J. Samuelson wrote about his own life on what he dubbed the "daddy track":

My wife fits the stereotype of someone on the mommy track. Since our daughter's birth four years ago, she's been in and out of part-time jobs. She now has a job three days a week. But she doesn't think she's made a "sacrifice." My wife got off whatever track she was on because she wanted to. When my daughter arrived, I didn't suddenly lose all ambition. But I started getting home earlier at night, working less on weekends, and deferring (forever?) some bigger and enticing writing projects. Both of us hope that what we're doing will help our children become more self-reliant and contented adults. Being a bit goofy, I'd like to think we're even helping the country in a small way by raising responsible and productive citizens. . . . We're doing what we're doing because we also think it's good for us. . . . My children are exasperating, exhausting, and exhilarating. They are the best part of me, and I won't miss their growing up.

Clarifying Values

Every action a person takes is based on the beliefs, attitudes, and values he holds. Some of these are conscious, some unconscious. Some are the result of experience and personal decision; others are influenced by society at large. The more that parents become consciously aware of what values are important to them, the more intelligently they can make choices and explain those choices to their children.

In the 1960s some social scientists and psychologists developed techniques for "values clarification," to help people identify their own priorities so that they could better deal with the great number of choices in their lives. One technique, called a values survey, involves listing values in order of priority.

Although there is no one set of values to which everyone will subscribe, most lists tend to overlap. When the Baltimore County public school system was creating a values curriculum, for instance, it looked to the United States Constitution and Bill of Rights as sources and came up with these merits and attributes: compassion, courtesy, critical inquiry, due process, equality of opportunity, freedom of thought and action, honesty, human worth and dignity, integrity, justice, knowledge, loyalty, objectivity, order, patriotism, rational consent, reasoned argument, respect for others' rights, responsible citizenship, rule of law, self-respect, tolerance, and truth.

The following is a list of "guiding principles" that was created by Milton Rokeach, one of the leaders in values research: a comfortable life (a prosperous life), equality (brotherhood, equal opportunity for all), an exciting life (a stimulating, active life), family security (taking care of loved ones), freedom (independence, free choice), happiness (contentedness), inner harmony (freedom from inner conflict), mature love (sexual and spiritual intimacy), national security (protection from attack), pleasure (an enjoyable, leisurely life), salvation (deliverance from sin, eternal life), self-respect (self-esteem), a sense of accomplishment (making a lasting contribution), social recognition (respect, admiration), true friendship (close companionship), wisdom (a mature understanding of life), a world at peace (freedom from war and conflict), a world of beauty (beauty of nature and the arts).

As a form of moral education, values clarification has been criticized for being neutral to an extreme. Most parents today would want to assert that some moral positions are better than others. They can still use the values survey technique with the lists above or one of their own to identify their values and priorities, and to help them explain to their children the reasons for decisions or policies they may have made. A discussion of differences might lead to an understanding of what lies behind family conflicts.

Less abstractly, parents can also discuss with their children how to act in situations in which values choices must be made. Depending on each child's age, topics could include whether to give money to a panhandler, what to do when a child takes money from a parent's wallet, how to act when everyone else is teasing another child, or how to handle unwelcome sexual advances from a boyfriend or girlfriend.

Parents should be prepared, however, for the possibility that some of their children's values, especially those of teenagers, may not always be the same as their own. In cases where they can accept this rather than lose communication with their children or have them act behind their backs, parents may choose to stress responsible and safe behavior, such as the use of birth control or calling for a ride home after drinking at a party.

Sharing Values

Although educators have developed a variety of systems for teaching children values and many parents are now clamoring for values education programs in the schools, there is no doubt that the primary transmitters of values to children are their mothers and fathers. In fact, long before public schools existed or psychologists began to study "moral judgment" or "prosocial behavior," the Bible enjoined parents to: "Train up a child in the way he should go, and even when he is old he will not depart from it" (Proverbs 22:6).

In their book *Bringing Up a Moral Child,* psychologists Michael Schulman, Ph.D., and Eva Mekler describe three "foundation stones of moral development" to guide parents in teaching morality to their children: internalizing parental standards of right and wrong action; developing empathic reactions to other people's feelings; and constructing personal standards of kindness and justice.

There are several direct ways that parents can help children internalize their standards and thus help them begin to develop a conscience. The most important is to be warm and loving. Very young children follow their parents' rules mainly because of love for them and the desire to please them. Moreover, children who feel secure in their parents' love are most able to give love back.

Children should know exactly what kind of behavior is valued by their parents. Rules should be clear and consistent. The consequences a child can expect when he fails to follow a rule should be clear, too. When children act well on their own, they should be praised. When they misbehave, the punishment should be fast and firm but not frightening. It should also be appropriate for the child's age. A 15-minute time-out, for example, can be just as effective for a three- or four-year-old as a half-hour time-out would be for a six-year-old.

Children can also be helped to understand the feelings of the victim. If a boy joins his friends in calling another boy "Fatso," for example, a parent might say, "Timmy probably is not happy about being overweight, and teasing him will make him feel worse." Attribution of good intentions is another powerful device, which can soften the criticism: "But I know you are the kind of person who usually cares about people's feelings. So maybe now you can think of a way to make him feel better."

Children need to understand the reasons behind rules in order to be able to make those rules their own and apply them to new situations. When two children are fighting over a toy, for instance, it is less helpful to say "Our rule is that you have to share" than "We share things with others because we want everyone to have a good time playing." Developing the habit of discussing these issues at an early age will pay off when children are older and sensitive moral issues abound, be they making choices about taking drugs or having compassion for the less fortunate.

Parents who want to pass their standards of right and wrong to their children also must be good role models. Studies have shown that children will be more generous and helpful if they see adults or another child behaving that way. Parents can reinforce their acts by stating in words what they are doing and why, and how good it makes them feel to be doing it ("I'm going to give up my seat on the bus because this older man getting on looks as if he isn't able to stand very well. I'm glad I can help him out").

Words alone are not enough, however. Moralizing to children tends to affect only what they say, not how they act. Children are too smart to buy the hypocritical line: "Do what I say, not what I do." Studies have shown that children are likely to choose what they see over what they are told. Parents need to make a conscious effort to live their lives according to the values they want for their children. Parents cannot lie about their children's ages in order to pay less for movie tickets, for instance, and then expect their children to have respect for the law.

Empathy, the second "foundation stone of moral development," is the ability to feel for others and to understand their point of view. Children are born with the capacity for empathy, though to varying degrees. As early as one year of age, or possibly even before, children begin to respond to the emotions of others. One way to help children develop empathy is for parents to teach them to pay attention to people's feelings. Parents must explain emotions to children—what causes them and how they relate to the way people act ("Uncle Ben is quiet on this visit because he's worried about Aunt Marie, who is in the hospital"). Asking a child to imagine how someone is feeling or to put himself in that person's place is often enough to elicit empathy.

Children will not feel empathy, however, for someone with whom they are angry or whom they think of as alien. Therefore, parents must teach their children to deal with their anger constructively, in other words, to let anger serve as a signal for starting a process of problem solving. With elementary-school–age children, role-playing—in which the parent plays the part of the person provoking the anger— can help them prepare for those situations.

Parents must encourage children to include all of humanity in their definition of "us." They can point out caring people and caring acts when they and their children encounter them—in books and movies and especially in real life—and praise their children for their own acts of sensitivity and kindness. Creating age-appropriate opportunities to practice caring, and teaching children the skills to carry them out are essential in fostering awareness and tolerance.

For instance, a parent might encourage a child to send a note along with a small gift he helped to choose for a classmate in the hospital, or help her sort through outgrown clothes and toys to give away. Compassionate behavior often leads to compassionate attitudes.

Finally, the way to foster the development of personal moral standards of kindness and justice (the third "foundation stone," according to Dr. Schulman and Mekler) is to persuade children, through logical arguments and concrete evidence, that living up to moral standards generally produces a good outcome. Acting morally is not always easy, especially when it goes against peer pressure, but parents can point out that it feels good to do good, and it benefits the community at large. Moral behavior often is also practical (violence, for instance, does not solve arguments). Parents should make this kind of behavior a requirement.

Dr. William Damon stresses the importance of encouraging children to assume responsibility by giving them responsibility. "Only through real service," he writes, "can children learn what it means to have others rely on them, to be entrusted with an important function, and to bear the credit or blame for a necessary job well or poorly done." In agrarian societies, and in America in earlier times, children did serious work on which their families' welfare depended. Parents today need to find a similar kind of experience for their children, appropriate to their age and abilities.

Children also should have opportunities to develop the skills for making their own decisions. Lawrence Kohlberg, Ph.D., a leading theorist of moral development, found that parents who encourage their children to express opinions, ideas, and suggestions; who discuss with them issues of right and wrong and the reasons for decisions that concern them; and who allow children to take part in family decisions are also helping them to develop moral and ethical principles.

Moral education, then, begins in earliest childhood. In their everyday social relationships children encounter issues of fairness, honesty, kindness, obedience, and responsibility. Very young children can learn the value of cooperation through games as simple as rolling a ball back and forth. When two children are both tugging at a book, they can be encouraged to look at it together. They can learn to be gentle with other children and with pets. By treating their children with respect—giving them choices and then honoring their decisions—parents teach respect for others. And by being honest and fair with them, they teach honesty and fairness.

Children between the ages of five and 12 can learn the values involved in being a friend and the ways to resolve conflicts constructively. They also can be given family responsibilities: for a pet or a sibling, or for age-appropriate household chores. Older children can learn, in addition, about the injustices in society. They should be taught how to help, however, not be made to feel guilty. By the time they are teenagers, children need to be able to make decisions and act on their own because they will frequently have to choose between right and wrong in the face of strong peer pressure.

The Generation Gap

Nowadays some parents feel that their moral lessons can hardly compete with all the conflicting messages children receive from the society around them. Newspaper headlines shout out stories of successful business people, sports heroes, and government officials who have cheated, lied, stolen, and used illegal drugs. Television, movies, and advertisements are filled with the glamour of drugs, sex, and violence. And in a grim but funny tale entitled "Material Girls and Boys" (*House and Garden*, October 1988), writer Delia Ephron demonstrates society's rampant materialism, exhibited in Los Angeles in perhaps its rawest form and mirrored by its children. She describes, for instance, a popular local car game called "That's mine!" Driving past the expensive houses, fancy cars, and lavish shops their parents idolize, L.A. kids shout out "That's mine!" Whoever shouts first wins, theoretically acquiring the desired object.

Children seem to be exposed to temptations and risks in greater numbers and at an earlier age than their parents were. And no longer are they sheltered from evil by a community united in its values.

Parents should not despair too quickly, however, for even in the face of such daunting opposition, they apparently have been holding their own. Based on findings of a recent study of 6,000 adolescents from 10 nations (including the United States), the Center for the Study of Adolescence in Chicago concluded that most adolescents are not alienated from their parents. According to one of the researchers, psychologist Robert Atkinson, Ph.D., "We found that today's youth have great respect for their parents. Very few teenagers expressed dislike for or carried grudges against their parents. Few thought their parents were ashamed of them, and almost all felt assured of their parents' continued support and pride in them."

When the sociologists who had studied "Middletown" (a pseudonym for Muncie, Indiana) in the 1920s and 1930s returned in 1976 and 1981 and asked the same questions they had asked 50 years earlier, they found that families had grown closer and that children's values were much like those of their parents. Finally, in spite of public concern about the fate of the family, 1985 surveys conducted by the Higher Education Research Institute of U.C.L.A. revealed that 70 percent of college freshmen described the goal of rearing a family as ''very important'' or ''essential.'' With this encouragement, parents should feel more confident in their ability to share their values with their children. The generation gap, many have found, often can be bridged by words.

PART II

······

Who We Are

CHAPTER THREE

• • • • • •

A Balancing Act: Family and Work

My mother was at home with the three of us when we were growing up. She did typical homemaking and house-keeping kinds of things. Every day when we came home from school we would sit down and have a snack and talk about the day. My friends used to come over and my mother played a lot of games with us: board games, word games of different kinds.

My life is very different. I worked until the day before my first daughter was born. I stopped working for a little over three years. Then I went back to work, managing the apart-ment complex where I live, when my second daughter was about three months old.

Working is important to me. I had a hard time with the idea of living entirely on money that my husband gave me. I worried about what I would do if my situation changed dramatically—if he died, for example. How would I get back into the working world and earn enough to support my fam-ily? Also, without my income, our lifestyle would be differ-ent. I think we would miss that.

I also realized that when I was at home I really wasn't spending a great deal of time with my children doing creative and enjoyable things. I was busy trying to get the housework done and attending to the basic needs of two small children.

I try to spend some time reading to each of my children every day, and we do play board games together occasionally as a family. But I have very little time for that. And I don't supervise my children's activities to the same extent that my mother did. I don't know their friends as my mother knew my friends. In many ways, I think that's the biggest void in my mothering.

I also feel as though I'm on a very tight schedule. The worst time is from 4:30 to about 7:00 at night. At work, everyone seems to call up with last-minute things. I realize what I didn't get done during the day that should be done before I leave. And even having no commuting time (my office is in the building where I live), I find it stressful to have to be home by a particular hour so the baby-sitter can leave on time.

And as soon as I walk in the door, I have two children who both want attention. I have to make dinner. The girls need to be bathed. During the school year my older daughter has homework. Usually she does it in the kitchen while I'm cooking dinner so that she can ask me questions or I can read spelling words to her. We all have dinner together. I spend a little time with them at bedtime reading or playing. Then my husband and I might sit down and have a cup of coffee and some dessert or watch a little television. But this is also the only time I have to do my personal paperwork.

My husband is more involved in the day-to-day issues of child rearing than my father was, but the baby-sitting arrangements, the doctors' appointments, the decision to buy new clothes, all those kinds of things I do. And I have more responsibility for the housework. It's not just because he works longer hours. I think it's more what we are accustomed to doing. If I had a job comparable to his, I suspect I'd still be doing the housework. All the women I know still do.

For me, the hardest part of being a working mother is the relentlessness of all the tasks. There seems to be very little flexible time in my day that I can just spend as I want to.

—A MOTHER

My father worked long hours when I was growing up, and when I was little he worked six days a week. But he is a nurturant person, and I always felt he was there for me. He just wasn't around that often. I do think that if he had been home more, my mother would have had more patience.

The way things are set up now, men work hard in their 20s and 30s and early 40s, and work less when they hit 45. Then we can spend more time at home. But that's when your kids are already grown. They're playing more with peers, and they're in school a longer time and busy with after-school activities. They don't have time to be with you and they don't want to be. What I would prefer is a reverse kind of option. And that's sort of how I see myself.

When my son was born, my wife and I shared child care about 50-50. Now my wife does more. During my son's first year, I took off from work to finish my dissertation and made myself available to him. My wife worked a lot during that time. She's a graphic designer. We shared the housework and cooking, as well as the bathing, feeding, putting to bed, diapering, and all those things. We still do that, but now we have a housekeeper who comes in a couple of days a week to help clean.

Sometimes that first year, my mother's comments would bother me when she called or visited. Even now, whenever she calls on a morning when I'm home, she'll be quiet first and then say, ''Oh . . . I'm just not used to hearing a man's voice in the morning during the week.'' I'm different from what she wants me to be. It's not that she doesn't want me to be nurturant, but my career is very important to her.

Meanwhile, my time at home has gradually decreased. In the morning I take my son to school, and I don't work on Fridays so I can be with him. I've tried to keep that going. I'm a psychologist, so I can make my schedule flexible. I know I could be giving more talks, seeing more clients, get-

ting more referrals, and working on becoming better known. But my philosophy is to wait for those things, to wait to work more when my son is older, even though I am sacrificing the money I might make.

I don't know what effect my being around more is going to have on him. I think some parents, men and women, don't like being with their kids. For me, being with my son is a pleasure.

—A FATHER

The two primary tasks of adulthood, according to Sigmund Freud, are love and work. What that translates into for many parents today is a 24-hour juggling act, as they try to keep three balls—jobs, children, and marriage or personal relationships—constantly in the air.

In 1950 only 12 percent of mothers with children younger than six were in the labor force. By 1988 this figure had risen to more than 57 percent, including 52 percent of mothers of children under three. Now, married women with children under three are entering the labor force in greater numbers than any other group. The United States Labor Department estimates that by the year 2000, 84 percent of women of childbearing age will be working.

Today's parents are hampered by business and government policies that are a generation behind the times. Jobs are still designed for men who have wives at home to raise their children and do their housework. Even though the United States has many laws and federal and state programs concerning families, it is the only industrialized nation in the world, except for South Africa, that doesn't have an explicit national family policy. Governments in Sweden, France, and Germany, for instance, have created policies, such as subsidizing child care, that help parents combine their family and work life. They also negotiate industrial benefits nationally with the concerns of working families in mind. United States policy has been much more scatter-shot. Federal laws affecting family life, such as taxes and welfare, change with administrations and are applied differently in each state. Employee benefits are negotiated by particular unions. U.S. families have suffered accordingly.

In her book *The Second Shift*, sociologist Arlie Hochschild describes our present state as a "stalled revolution." "The work force has changed," she writes. "Women have changed. But most workplaces have remained inflexible in the face of the family demands of their workers, and at home most men have yet to really adapt to the changes in women."

Most working mothers—and fathers—also often lack role models in their parents' generation for the kinds of lives they are leading. They didn't grow up seeing their mothers and fathers make smooth transitions between work and home, able to fulfill the demands of both. In the 1946 edition of *Dr. Spock's Baby and Child Care*, the bestselling bible of child-care advice, Benjamin Spock, M.D., warned that "it doesn't make much sense to have mothers go to work and have them pay other people to do a poorer job of bringing up their children." However, 30 years later he wrote, "Both parents have an equal right to a career if they want one, and an equal obligation to share in the care of their children." That sounds great on paper, but no one has told parents how to accomplish it.

Traditionally, balancing work and family has been considered a woman's problem. There is a magazine called *Working Mother*, for instance, but none called *Working Father* or even *Caring Father*. As long ago as 1919 the *Smith College Weekly* published this statement for its alumnae: "We cannot believe that it is fixed in the nature of things that a woman must choose between a home and her work, when a man may have both. There must be a way out and it is the problem of our generation to find the way." In 1925 Smith set up the Institute to Coordinate Women's Interests, which experimented with cooperative nurseries, communal laundries, shopping groups, and central kitchens. Unfortunately the Great Depression put an end to this, and the problem was passed unsolved to the next generation, and the next.

However, men, too, are feeling the strain of dual roles. In a *New York Times* poll conducted in June 1989, 72 percent of working fathers as well as 83 percent of working mothers complained of the conflict between the demands of their jobs and their desire to spend time with their families. In another survey, done in the summer of 1989 for the recruiting firm Robert Half International, 56 percent of the men said they would sacrifice as much as one-quarter of their salary for more family or personal time; 45 percent said they would probably refuse a promotion that required more hours away from their families.

Clearly many parents today, whatever their values and beliefs about working and raising a family, are frustrated in their desire to act upon them. Even those (like the mother and father quoted at the beginning of this chapter) who can arrange individual solutions often have to compromise. The mother describes sacrificing the deep knowledge and direction of her children's lives that her mother had had; the father describes losing income and career advancement. Emotionally and financially, many other parents feel stretched thin when their work and love needs pull them simultaneously in two different directions.

Although we are far from arriving at a universal solution, the work-family problem at least is being acknowledged now. There are a few hopeful, though small, signs of social change. Parents are beginning to demand family benefits. Business and government are beginning to respond as they realize that employees who are parents are more productive when they do not have to worry about child care. According to an October 3, 1988, *Time* magazine article, more than half of American firms that year gave some form of maternity leave, 10 percent gave some child-care assistance, and about 60 percent offered employees some choice in their hours, allowing them to come earlier or later so long as they worked a full day. In addition, at the end of 1990, Congress finally passed two pieces of legislation aimed at increasing the availability and quality of child care, one of which is targeted to poor working families. As of this writing, the House is considering two bills, though experts predict the need for a House-Senate conference to decide on final legislation.

Because of the growing number of women in the work force and the labor shortage predicted for the 1990s, neither government nor business will be able to ignore the needs of working parents much longer. The trend for the future seems to be some government subsidy of day care and a range of corporate benefits for working parents, including possible on-site child care, emergency child-care assistance, part-time work sharing, more flexible hours, and increased home-based employment. Employees who are able to take advantage of these options, however, need to insist that they also retain the benefits that previous generations fought hard to secure.

Working Mothers

Today 70 percent of working mothers say that they need to work for economic reasons. Women also cannot ignore the divorce statistics and the all-too-real possibility that they may one day find themselves the sole support of a family.

Even though most women with custody of children after a divorce are legally entitled to child support, very few divorced fathers make regular payments. Some pay for a time, then stop. Enforcement of these payments through legal action has, at present, a low success rate. Women therefore no longer see themselves as working just until they get married. In 1959 men on the average were in the work force 30 years longer than women. Now the difference has shrunk to only 10 years.

Despite their greater presence in the work force, women are still concentrated in lower-paying jobs. They generally earn only about 70 percent of what men earn, and only a few rise to very high levels in business. In about 80 percent of two-job couples, the man earns more. One explanation is the continued imbalance in the division of labor at home. Most men can concentrate their full energies on succeeding at work; they don't have to worry about producing costumes overnight for their children's school plays, or even washing their own underwear or ironing their own shirts. Most women still have two jobs: the one at work and the one at home, of which costumes, underwear, and shirts are only a small part. This helps to explain why 95 percent of male executives have children and only 40 percent of women executives do, and why a frequent cry heard from women workers is "I need a wife!"

Sociologist Arlie Hochschild, Ph.D., coined the term *second shift* for the work that women with jobs do at home. She calculated that the average working mother clocks about 15 hours more work per week than does her husband in combined job and homemaking duties. Over the course of a year this amounts to an extra month of 24-hour days. Dr. Hochschild also found that even when couples share the burden of housework more equally, women do two-thirds of the daily, routine jobs, such as cooking and cleaning up, and often have to do two things at once (preparing dinner and supervising homework, for instance, like the woman who was quoted at the beginning of this chapter). Women also devote more of their at-home time to housework than to child care; for men the bigger demand on their at-home time is child care.

Many working mothers suffer a tremendous burden of guilt at not living up to the 1950s myth of what a mother should be like. They feel guilty that they cannot be with their children all the time, that their housekeeping is slipshod, that their substitute child care is not good enough. They even feel guilty when their children's behavior shows the ups and downs of normal development. And should anything truly go awry for their children, others are often only too eager to wag their fingers at the working mother. Why does Jan have trouble in school? Because her mother works, of course. What about all the children who are having school problems whose mothers are at home? And what about Jan's working father? He is not likely to be made to feel guilty. Men are more likely to congratulate themselves for whatever they do to help things go right than to castigate themselves for what they didn't do when things go wrong.

It is evident that despite the growing number of mothers in the work force, our society still expresses much ambivalence about working mothers. In a 1986 *Newsweek* magazine survey, 57 percent of at-home mothers and 59 percent of working mothers said that it is less socially acceptable today to stay home with children. Yet many working mothers feel envious of mothers who are at home with their children while they simultaneously feel superior to them. Some experts see a rising antagonism between mothers at work and mothers at home.

Another sign of ambivalence about a woman's role is the number of women who are unwilling to give up their traditional dominance in the home in exchange for more help from their husbands. In a 1980 survey of working women, Joseph Pleck, Ph.D., at the Wellesley College Center for Research on Women found that fewer than half wanted their husbands to help more with child care and only a little over a third wanted them to do more housework. Other studies show that women's attitudes affect how much child care their husbands do and refer to women as the ''gate-keepers'' of men's participation.

The conflict for women today, then, is more than one between being a mother and having a career. As Sandra Scarr, professor of psychology at the University of Virginia, wrote in *Mother Care/Other Care*, ''The dilemmas of modern motherhood arise from a mismatch between the current realities of family life and ideas about mothers and children that suited the late nineteenth and early twentieth centuries.''

In the 1990s one clear message blares to working mothers: Down with Superwoman! Both women and men have come to accept that it is simply impossible for a woman to be Margaret Thatcher, Donna Reed, and Julia Child all in one. The advice from working women today to their younger sisters and older daughters is ''Don't try to do it all.'' When a son needs a hug or a daughter needs extra help with her homework, the kitchen floor may not get its regular mopping. But every sticky footstep will be a reminder of the things that really matter.

The only way for women to ''have it all'' without doing it all is to enlist and insist upon the help of their husbands and children. Sharing the load benefits everyone; men expand their definition of manhood, and children learn responsibility and competence. A more expensive solution is to pay others to do as many of the time-consuming household chores as a family can afford. The restaurant industry, for instance, is one institution that has responded imaginatively to the needs of working parents, offering varieties of take-out food that range from burgers to full-course meals. If getting outside help isn't possible, parents need to lower their standards and reorder their priorities. "By the time I get home," one hardworking mother said, "it's too dark for me to see the dust on the furniture anyway."

Especially during the early years, when children require an extraordinary amount of sheer physical energy, mothers and fathers also may have to accept remaining at a temporary plateau in their careers. In the January/February 1989 issue of the *Harvard Business Review*, Felice Schwartz, founder of Catalyst, a research and advisory organization, recommended that companies offer a separate, slower career track (dubbed the "mommy track") to women who want to combine career and family. These women would sacrifice advancement and some income in exchange for more time with their children. Although this proposal was originally criticized as giving companies an excuse to discriminate against women, now some men are campaigning for a "parent track." Schwartz believes that careers can develop in stages as well as on a straight path and that companies that won't accept this idea may find themselves with a shortage of experienced workers.

Meanwhile, there are some strategies that working mothers can use to reduce the stress of their two roles. For the sake of themselves and their families, they need to be able to compartmentalize, to leave work problems at the office door and, to some degree, to leave their home lives behind them on the front porch. Some mothers arrive at work 10 minutes early to read a newspaper and have a quiet cup of coffee. For some, clearing their desk at the end of the day is a signal to shut down. Some mothers take the long route home on particularly harrowing days to try to walk off the tension before they see their children. Some use their commute to unwind by listening to music tapes or reading for pleasure. Some relax by diving into the shower or drinking a cup of tea as soon as they get home. Others may allow 10 or 15 minutes to catch up on the day's events, then demand a little quiet time to catch their breath. This may be when they assign dinnertime jobs or allow children to watch a television show.

In addition, working mothers of children of any age need regular personal time, to be alone and to be with their spouses or friends. This may mean a grown-ups-only dinner out, an exercise class, or a bowling league—whatever refreshes them. Treating oneself well as a person helps anyone be a better parent. The guiding principle is that working mothers need "quality time" just as much as their children do.

Perhaps it will take another generation before society is completely comfortable with women's new roles. The children of today's working mothers will have different models from those of their own mothers and fathers and probably will not be so heavily burdened with guilt and ambivalence about how to expend their limited time and energy. Based on the studies done so far, they may also have enjoyed some benefits from their mothers' employment outside the home and may themselves see a clearer path to balancing family and work. By then, too, the workplace is likely to have responded better to the needs of working parents.

Caregiving Fathers

Men are burdened with outdated notions of their role as parents that interfere with their ability to be nurturing. The message many men traditionally receive is that their domain is limited to ensuring the financial security of the family. Real men, they learn, express their love for their children indirectly by providing for, protecting, and guiding them. In fact, some men's "natural" response to the birth of a child is to work longer and harder in order to be even better providers and, thus, better fathers.

The work world reinforces this belief by rewarding qualities contrary to those that children require in parents. While children need warmth and attachment, successful workers are usually competitive, efficient, and emotionally detached. They also devote much time and energy to their jobs. Men who choose to take time off to be with their babies are often treated with suspicion by their colleagues and superiors and considered unserious or even unmanly. Society can much more readily accept women who aspire to traditionally male roles than men who aspire to roles that are traditionally female.

There have been some signs of change, however, both in fathers' values and in their willingness to admit them. In a 1989 survey of its employees, the Du Pont Corporation found that many more fathers of school-age children were interested in flexible hours and paternity leave than had been the case only four years earlier.

In his book *The Nuturing Father*, Kyle D. Pruett, M.D., identified some of the most salient experiences for men who become active fathers. He advises fathers to get involved with their children even before birth. An expectant couple should choose a clinic or obstetrician together so that the man will have an equal chance to ask questions and express concerns. The father should participate in childbirth classes as well as those on the physical care and feeding of a baby. For most fathers, the experience of being present at the birth of their child is a high point in their lives. By the time the baby leaves the hospital, the father should know how to diaper, bottle-feed, and bathe her.

The first three months of a baby's life can be a critical time, when fathers either turn on or turn off to child rearing. This period has been called the fourth trimester because some women treat their babies as if they were still part of their bodies. Yet this is just the time when fathers should be gaining confidence as caregivers. Fathers and mothers should talk openly about their rivalries over their baby, which are normal during this time, so that the father is not excluded.

Studies by sociology professor Norma Radin, M.S.W., Ph.D., at the University of Michigan have shown that children of highly involved fathers are better adjusted socially and emotionally and do better on some academic tests than do children of uninvolved fathers. Possible explanations include fathers' distinct styles of handling children and the simple benefits of being exposed to two different nurturing styles and of receiving the attention of two parents instead of the usual one and a half.

In the past, traditional fathers tended to reinforce sex-role stereotypes. They encouraged independence and mastery of tasks with their sons while discouraging emotional expression. They reversed the emphasis with their daughters. There is some evidence now that more nurturing fathers help both boys and girls retain their feminine and masculine sides. Although a long-term effect has not yet been proven, these fathers may be playing an important part in shaping the nature of fathers' roles in the future, at home and at work.

How Children Are Affected

"You know what's weird about Mrs. Piggle-Wiggle?" a seven-year-old boy recently asked his mother, who had been reading him the series of humorous children's books written in the 1950s. "None of the mothers have jobs. They always stay in the kitchen after the kids go to school." For this child, the 1950s might as well have been the Middle Ages. While his mother is struggling to reconcile her present desires as a mother with her past conditioning as a child, her child is living in the here and now.

Obviously, children whose mothers have jobs have different experiences from those whose mothers are at home, but some of those differences are not as striking as one might assume. According to Sandra Scarr, Ph.D., in *Mother Care/Other Care*, time-use studies show that working mothers spend as much time in direct interaction (talking, playing, and reading) with their children as do mothers at home, though they are physically present much less. Perhaps more surprising is the statistic she cites that this direct interaction generally amounts to only 5 percent of a child's waking hours.

Since the 1930s there have been numerous studies of the effects of mothers' employment on their children. Based on a thorough review of this research, Ellen Galinsky, copresident, Families and Work Institute, and Judy David, Ed.D., of the Bank Street College of Education in New York City concluded in *The Preschool Years* that "children are not necessarily harmed or helped by the fact that their mothers are employed and they are cared for by others. The impact of a mother's employment depends; it depends upon the children's experiences in their families and in their child-care situations."

Nevertheless, there is at least the potential for a number of positive and negative effects. Experts who studied attachment, according to Galinsky and Dr. David, have found that while young children can become attached to a number of different people, their primary attachment is still to their parents. They also have found no difference in the strength of the attachment between children and mothers at home and those who work after the first year.

The major controversy is over children who are less than a year old. Jay Belsky, Ph.D., professor of psychology at Penn State University, and others have reported that infants whose mothers were away more than 20 hours a week during their first year were more likely to have insecure attachments to them. A number of researchers have questioned the meaning of these findings. In 1987 a group of experts met at the National Center for Clinical Infant Programs and issued this statement in response: "When parents have choices about selection and utilization of supplementary care for their infants and toddlers and have access to stable child-care arrangements featuring skilled, sensitive, and motivated caregivers, there is every reason to believe that both children and families can thrive." Of course, such high-quality child care is frequently unavailable, so that at present, no one knows what is the general effect on infants of mothers' employment outside the home.

Only recently have researchers begun to focus on the positive effects working mothers can have on children older than a year. In her 1984 review of the research, Lois Hoffman, Ph.D., professor of psychology at the University of Michigan, concluded that for girls, working mothers offer a model of competence. The daughters of working mothers, she found, are more self-confident, get better grades, and are more likely to choose careers. Both sons and daughters are also more independent and reliable.

Studies of other effects on sons are not as clear as those on daughters, reporting conflicting positive, negative, and neutral effects. On the positive side, the sons of working mothers show better social and personal adjustment. Negative effects differ according to class. In several studies of middle-class working families, the boys seemed to perform less well in the early years of elementary school than did those from traditional homes. In working-class families, the boys with working mothers did better in elementary school than did those with mothers at home, but their relationships with their fathers seemed to be more strained. To some experts these contradictory and as yet unexplained findings indicate the influence of other factors. The most important of these, according to Galinsky and Dr. David, are the mother's and family's attitudes toward her employment, stress from the mother's and father's jobs, other stressful events in the family, and the quality of substitute care provided for the children.

Some researchers report that when mothers feel satisfied with their work, believing that it is important to their family's finances or to their own well-being, the children identify with that good feeling and share it. Mothers who are effective role models talk to their children about what they do. There is no reason for a mother to feel guilty about admitting to her children that she enjoys working, nor should parents hide from their child some of the problems encountered on the job. By hearing how adults handle the demands and frustrations of work, children learn important lessons for their own lives. By hearing about their parents' jobs, they also gain a sense of the value of working.

In any one family, of course, more important than whether or not a mother works is the *quality* of her relationship with her children. One daughter of a working mother, now one herself, remembers resenting her mother's job not because it kept her away from home but "because she always told us that we came first but we always knew that we didn't. I never wanted my kids to feel that way. I don't censor their phone calls to me during the day and I try not to bring my work home."

Back to Work

Some women—and men—are able to choose when to return to work after their children are born. Some can arrange to work part-time or at home. Some can arrange to share a job with their spouse or another worker or, if their jobs have flexible shifts, can dovetail their schedules so that at least one parent is at home during most of the child's waking hours. Although choosing these options often means financial and career sacrifices, such alternatives are still attractive to some parents of young children. They should be attractive to employers also. Studies have found that part-time workers generally are more productive, are more loyal, are absent less, and, of course, cost less in salary and benefits. Yet few permanent part-time niches exist in the working world, and parents who want to create their own must apply great amounts of both imagination and persuasion.

For all workers, especially the majority who have traditional full-time jobs, an important question is, When is the best time to go back to work after the birth of a child? According to pediatrician and child development expert T. Berry Brazelton, M.D., in his book *Working and Caring*, the best time is generally when the child is not mastering a new cognitive or motor skill. An eight-month-old who is struggling to crawl, for instance, will not be able to tolerate stress as well as she would a month later, when she is an adept crawler. Four-and-a-half months, eight months, and 12 to 16 months are often periods of stranger anxiety—fear of new people and new places—and thus bad times to introduce a substitute caregiver. At one year, babies are beginning to walk or cruise and may be wary of this new independence.

The decision of when to return to work is essentially a personal one, but some experts believe that the first year of life is so developmentally important that a parent should be there full-time. Dr. Brazelton recommends that mothers (and fathers, if possible) stay at home with their babies for at least the first four months. He is now working to institute a national policy that would guarantee at least a four-month paid leave for working mothers and fathers. Brazelton contends that in four months mothers, fathers, and babies have time to attach to each other and will have enjoyed a playful period together. By then parents usually know how to make their baby laugh and how to handle the crying jags, and they are more confident by then that the baby knows who they are. At four months, she probably is interested in exploring the world and may be ready for new experiences and meeting new adults.

Because returning to work can be a wrenching emotional experience, Dr. Brazelton's proposed national policy would allow parents to return gradually. Even if this is impossible, which it often is, he encourages mothers who enjoy breast-feeding not to abandon it. If a baby is nursed three times a day—in the morning, at the end of the work day, and late at night—the mother's milk will keep flowing. "Having nursing to look forward to at the end of a working day makes for a happy and very meaningful reunion," he notes.

Mothers sometimes feel guilty because their children regress, that is, act in more immature ways, when they return to work. This is a normal reaction for children of any age to a change in their lives. If the child is treated gently and with understanding, the behavior should soon disappear.

Goings and Comings

Transitions—leaving for work and coming home—are probably the hardest times for working parents and their children. But there are some simple ways to ease them.

Mornings and Leave-takings

Since mornings set the tone for the day, they should be as relaxed and pleasant as possible. If parents find themselves always rushing and the children always dawdling, they should plan to get everyone up 10 or 15 minutes earlier to avoid the battle. Some parents of older children even allow a time to exercise together early in the morning.

With younger children, waking up should be a playful, social time. In their book *The Woman Who Works, the Parent Who Cares,* Sirgay Sanger, M.D., an infant psychiatrist, and writer John Kelly recommend that one morning activity be left unfinished until parents return at night. During the day, whenever the child sees the half-built farm or half-finished puzzle, she will be reminded that her parents are going to return, and will be comforted by her memory of them.

Breakfast itself should be a happy time, even if that means it is messier and less nutritious than the ideal meal. Too many parents, especially working parents, mistakenly judge the quality of their parenting by what is easily measurable: vitamins ingested, or worse, scores on standardized tests. But often children assert their independence at mealtimes. For some parents of young children, the best policy is to make lunch the major meal of the day, as it is in many other countries. Passing the buck to the caregiver in this way takes the pressure off breakfast and supper, so that these times can be enjoyable ones for the family. With teenagers, a temporary diet of mayonnaise and potato-chip sandwiches is a fairly harmless form of rebellion and should probably be indulged.

Homecomings and Bedtimes

Children often seem to fall apart when their parents pick them up from day care or return home from work. It is as if they were saving up their feelings all day—and maybe they are. Rather than rush immediately to the kitchen to prepare dinner, some working mothers instead serve a quick snack (carrots dipped in peanut butter are popular hors d'oeuvres in one household). Family members can get reacquainted and talk about their day for a while without suffering hunger pangs.

When children become wild at the end of the day, some working parents have trouble disciplining them. Tired and lonely for their children all day, they don't want to spoil any of their precious time together. Usually, however, children who misbehave are glad to have limits set for them. They will reward their parents' efforts by eventually learning self-discipline.

Most evenings for working parents feature a period of *quality time.* This term is often misunderstood to mean cramming a full day's stimulation into two hours. Dr. Sanger points out, however, that young children prefer events that are relaxed, open-ended, and spontaneous. He recommends allowing children to follow their own interests at their own pace and offering no more than two or three activities in an evening. If children want to watch television, parents should watch with them and talk about the programs they see. If there are two or more siblings, each child should have some time alone with each parent, if not every night then at least every week. If this time has been scheduled, the parent can refer to it (''We'll talk about planning your birthday party tomorrow night when we have our special time together''), and the child can look forward to it.

Finally, saying good night—putting children to bed and keeping them there—is also often difficult for parents who have been away all day. Hour-long bedtime rituals and playtimes in the middle of the night, however, are not good for either parent or child. Both need their sleep to function well the next day. Learning to sleep through the night also is an important step in a child's developing sense of independence.

In-Between Times

The telephone is the working parents' greatest ally. A mid-morning call, if possible, can reassure a young child that her mother and father are thinking about her even if they are far away. School-age children yearn for this contact, too. For their book *The Working Parent Dilemma,* Rabbi Earl Grollman and Gerri Sweder surveyed about 1,000 children of working parents. Fourth graders through high-school students stated "emphatically" that they wanted to talk to their parents after school. These phone calls from parents not only remind children that they are always on their parents' minds but also help to ease the loneliness and anxiety they may feel while they are separated.

Travel and Business Trips

If parents must travel for business, the best way they can help their children through the separation is by calling home daily. They also can leave behind comforting reminders of themselves. Young children might enjoy listening to a tape each night of Mom or Dad reading a favorite story. Children also like to count the days until a parent's return. Older children can mark the time off on a calendar and/or follow the travel route on a map. Younger children could select one cookie each night from a box that will be empty when the parent comes home. And children of all ages love a surprise bag filled with one present to open each night until the parent's return.

Dr. Sanger encourages parents of children under four to include them on vacations of more than two days. This time together, he writes, helps to build a sense of family. To ensure quality time for the grown-ups, parents can arrange for a baby-sitter some evenings or bring along a mother's helper. If parents need more than two days alone together to refuel their marriage, they might prepare their children by taking a few short trips without them before going away for a week. During longer trips they should try to arrange for children to be cared for at home, where they will feel most secure.

When parents return from any trip, aching for hugs and

kisses from their beloved children, they should prepare to be temporarily rejected. This is a normal way for children to express their anger at having been left behind and to assert some control.

A Time for Work and a Time for Play

The worst problem for working parents is time. There simply are not enough hours in a day. Yet children need some time set aside for them when they can talk and their parents can listen with full attention. In the evening, the phone may be an enemy rather than an ally. Some families take it off the hook for a while after dinner and before doing the dishes. Others use the quiet time before the children go to bed. Some time for family events also should be reserved during the weekends. For children in two-job families, according to Dr. Sanger, full-family activities reinforce their sense of themselves as part of a larger group, a sense which they sometimes lack.

Parents can also make a virtue of necessity. If school is out on a weekday, a parent may be able to bring a child to work. This will give the child a mental image of what her parent does during the day. If a child is sick enough to stay home from school or day care and her parent has to take the day off to look after her, the two of them could try to make it a cozy time by playing quiet games and talking and reading together. Parents should be careful, however, not to be too indulgent on these occasions, lest their child, consciously or unconsciously, come to prefer the sickbed to a day at school.

Another way to create time together is to incorporate it into the performance of daily chores. Helping to prepare dinner can be an exciting challenge for young children, who are eager to identify with their parents. Although the preparation will not be nearly as efficient, it can transform the mundane act of scraping carrots or snapping beans into a memorable event. Giving chores to children, in fact, can benefit the whole family. Not only does it reduce the parents' workload but it offers children the opportunity and reward of developing a sense of competence and contributing to the family's welfare.

It is important, however, to assign only those chores that are within a child's ability and not to overburden her. A young child may need to use scaled-down equipment and to have her task broken down into short, easy steps. An older child should not be doing the bulk of the housework. Rabbi Grollman and Sweder found from their questionnaires that many children feel overwhelmed by household responsibilities. By age 10, children often have homework and obligations to sports groups. At this age they also need some time to be alone or with their friends.

Some families assign chores at a family meeting so that there can be choices and everyone can agree about what is fair and what will happen if the chores are not done. Many families also rotate the least desirable chores.

As strange as it may seem, the practical demands of life in a two-job or single-parent family are often an asset for children. Through their contributions to the family enterprise, they can feel truly needed and valued.

CHAPTER FOUR

• • • • • •

Bringing Up Baby: Child-Care Choices

I was in the army, based in Kansas, when my daughter was born. I had to go back to work after only six weeks, so I had to find day care for this tiny, tiny baby. I was a single mother without any family and not very much money. I couldn't afford the private center, and they didn't take children as small as mine anyway.

I finally did find an army wife, a friend of a friend, who had older children. She seemed nice enough, but every time I went away for a field trip, my daughter would end up in the emergency room throwing up. So I always had to wonder what was going on. She moved away, and then I left Jessica with a woman who had eight kids, who seemed to work out much better.

After six months, I left the army and moved to New York City. I found two places that had infant day care, but one had a five-year waiting list and the other cost more than I could possibly pay. I didn't even have a job. I ended up applying to the city for subsidized day care and was on a waiting list for almost a year. I wasn't able to work until I got day care, so I was a welfare mother.

Finally, I was given the names of two different family day-care women. The first one lived in a housing project where the elevators smelled as though people used them for bathrooms. When we came in, the woman was sitting, watching television. She had sheets covering her sofa, and Jessica tripped over a torn sheet. The woman didn't even get up to move it. She was glued to the TV.

The other woman, Louisa, was one of those exceptional, dedicated people. When we visited her, another little girl was there. The little girl did something she wasn't supposed to and Louisa corrected her in such a nice, warm, loving way. Her apartment was very well kept up, very clean. Louisa's 77 now, and she's taken care of hundreds of kids. We still see her, and she still writes to Jessica, calls her, and sends her birthday cards.

When Jessica was three, I wanted her to be in a place where she'd have more contact with children, things to do, things to play with. I talked to a lot of people and luckily found an all-day nursery school with a sliding-fee scale, where she was very happy. For holidays and vacations she went back to Louisa.

Now Jessica's in school until 3:00. Although her school is free, I have to pay for the program she attends after school and during vacations. So I'm still in debt.

—A MOTHER

When my son was born, I stayed home for three months and then I went back to work. With my daughter I stayed home four months because I had vacation time. We've always had a baby-sitter in our house. I recommend this wholeheartedly if you can afford it. I never considered day care because I really felt that for the first year of my child's life I did not want him or her to be dragged elsewhere. And being a working mother and running a household, I also needed that extra help at home. My baby-sitters may not have done heavy cleaning, but they made the beds and kept my house neat. They also shopped for us and cooked for the children.

We've had three baby-sitters in nine years. Anne was with us for seven years. After she went to school to become a nurse's aide, Yvonne was with us for a year and a half.

When she moved to Florida to live with her daughter, we hired Barbara. For times in-between we had temporaries, either from agencies or grandparents filling in.

Occasionally we've gotten stuck. Anne had a health condition and she tended to get sick. If that happened on the spur of the moment, my husband and I split the days.

What is most important to us in a baby-sitter, besides taking good care of the children and being responsible, is that we want somebody who we feel can communicate easily with us. We had that with Anne, but with Yvonne it was difficult. We told her that we wanted our daughter to play with other children, but she didn't arrange much. Our son also walked all over her. He acted up with her and had tantrums. We needed someone firmer.

With a baby-sitter, it's a two-way street. I'm always really careful not to take advantage; we get home on time, for instance, even though it's difficult. And if I can't get home, it's usually planned ahead of time and we pay extra or I get another sitter, which is expensive. We've always believed that if you treat people well, they will treat you well. And so far we haven't been burned.

—A MOTHER

We decided we didn't want a caregiver or day-care home where Hannah would just be allowed to exist in a fairly warm situation. Her problem isn't getting love. Warmth and love she gets endlessly as an only child of parents who "smother" and "sfather" her. Her problem is having people who can keep up with her and help her gain a sense of responsibility, a sense that the world doesn't center around her. We thought that a more professionally oriented place made sense. And we thought she was ready at a year and a half. This kid is very extroverted. We had a harder transition than she did.

The first thing I assessed in day-care centers was the

teachers—the pride or joy they take in being teachers and their self-confidence. We liked the center we chose the first time we saw it. It was very intimate and the director ran it like a home. Most of the kids stay from 8 in the morning until 6. I usually pick up Hannah at 3, when I finish working, but I have that cushion if I need it.

I've become a believer in the validity of day care. Hannah has so clearly flourished there and made so many friends. There are also lots of things that are good for children to do that my wife and I simply don't enjoy doing. For instance, I recognize that drawing and pasting and glueing are wonderful activities for children. There's also a great richness to the design of a preschool. They are constantly designing curricula for the children. If you fall asleep at the wheel for a couple of weeks, the school wakes you up to the fact that your child's ready for something else now.

—A FATHER

For working parents, happiness often is not the perfect job but rather the near-perfect child-care situation. In a three-year study of 200 working mothers, researchers at the Columbia University School of Social Work reported that finding satisfactory child care was a source of constant stress for all of them. Mothers tend to bear most of the burden of making the child-care arrangements, ensuring their success, and filling the gap when they fail. "When my baby-sitter left for vacation and didn't return, I was paralyzed. I thought I would have to quit my job," says one working mother. "Between my sicknesses and my daughter's, I've been home from work a lot and I've been criticized for it. But what am I supposed to do? She hasn't even had chicken pox yet."

Unfortunately there is not enough high-quality child care in the United States to go around. Federal aid has been blocked in the past by a belief shared by many congressional representatives that young children should be cared for only at home by their mothers and by a fear that supporting any alternatives would encourage the breakdown of the family. Moreover, in the past, day-care policy bore negative connotations because it was tied to welfare. Only recently has day care reemerged as a middle-class concern, which has caught the ear of politicians and government administrators alike.

In the United States, day-care centers first appeared about 150 years ago during the Industrial Revolution to serve mothers working in factories. These were run by private charities and offered mainly custodial care, which meant just keeping the children safe and fed. The first public day-care centers were set up during the Great Depression to provide work for unemployed teachers, nurses, cooks, and janitors. During World War II, many more day-care centers were opened so that women could enter the work force, thus replacing the men who had left to fight. There were more than 1.5 million children in 2,800 day-care centers. After the war was over, when mothers once again remained at home, most of the centers closed.

Child Care Today

Not until the mid-1960s, with the increasing employment of women, was there another mass demand for day care. The number of centers doubled between 1967 and 1970. Day-care homes also started to boom. Many of these offered programs to promote children's social, intellectual, and emotional development.

Today the Urban Institute, a research group in Washington, D.C., has estimated that about 11 million children under the age of six have mothers in the work force. Of these, about 48 percent are cared for by relatives, 23 percent are in day-care centers, 22 percent are in family–day-care homes, and 6 percent are at home with caregivers.

Although Congress funded two child-care programs to begin in 1991, the United States still lags far behind many European countries whose governments have long supported women's right to work by providing the child care to make that possible. Many other countries have national child-care policies, some of which include more than subsidized day care. In Sweden, for instance, day care is available from early morning to early evening, even for infants. In addition, every working couple is entitled to 12 months of parental leave when a baby is born, to be divided as they choose. For nine months they receive 90 percent of their salary and for the last three, about $300 a month. Working parents with children under the age of eight can choose to limit their work day to six hours at six hours' pay. Parental insurance pays for work time lost due to caring for sick children or attending school appointments. The cost of such programs is reflected in a tax rate that is nearly 20 percent higher than what Americans pay. But the benefits are evident in the fact that, when questioned, parents in Sweden and West Germany do not understand the stress that Americans suffer by trying to balance commitments to work and family.

The United States also lags behind other industrialized nations in encouraging companies to provide day-care help for their employees. The Conference Board, a business research group based in New York City, estimated in Spring 1990 that 5,400 large U.S. employers (with more than 100 employees) offer child-care benefits. Three types of benefits were considered: on-site day care, child-care assistance and referral, and dependent-care (financial) assistance plans. Although this is a vast increase from the 110 firms counted in 1978, or even the 3,300 in 1988 it is still probably more than 15 percent of the total.

On-site or near-site day-care centers are now offered by nearly 200 corporations, 500 hospitals, and 50 government agencies. The benefit of this option for employees is that they can spend more time with their children. They travel back and forth together, and some parents also are able to visit their children briefly during the workday. Many employers believe that on-site day care reduces absenteeism and stress and increases productivity. An Indiana-based auto parts firm, for example, 85 percent of whose employees are women, was able to reduce its more than 100 percent annual turnover rate to 11 percent by providing a 24-hour learning center for workers' children. On-site care has proven successful also in hospitals, where the majority of workers are often women with varied schedules who need day care at times when it may not be available elsewhere.

On the other hand, many parents do not enjoy a daily commute with their children. They also worry about losing their child care if they quit or lose their jobs. Some companies, too, shy away from on-site day care because it requires a major fixed investment.

Parents' Needs

Parents today have a wide range of child-care needs, which they meet in a variety of ways. In some families one parent stays home while the children are young, though this may be a financial sacrifice. For them, outside child care may be needed infrequently and can be arranged informally either with relatives or by hiring teenagers or elderly people in the neighborhood for a few hours a week or on some evenings. Other parents juggle their work schedules so that one of them is at home during most of their children's waking hours. This usually requires a great deal of stamina, jobs with flexible hours, and a loss of marital time together. These parents also may need occasional help filling in the gaps when schedules do not overlap. Families with older children may need child care only for those after-school hours before working parents return home.

Increasingly, however, more and more parents with younger and younger children are looking for full-time child care. The three most common types available today are family day care, which is usually a caregiver with five or six children in her home; day-care centers, which have many more children, usually grouped by age; and in-home caregivers, who come to the child's home or live there, and may also do some housekeeping.

The type of full-time child care used by parents is determined by financial, personal, and employment considerations. Family day care might be the right choice for a single working mother on a tight budget. She might be unable to afford in-home care, usually the most expensive option. She also might want her child to develop a close relationship with another adult and to be in a family atmosphere with other children of varying ages. Other parents may value the stability a day-care center offers, since it is more likely to be licensed and less likely to curtail its services suddenly. Day-care centers also may handle a wider age range, thus providing a longer-term solution. Parents whose jobs require travel and overtime might prefer the kind of flexible arrangement more often possible with family day care or an in-home caregiver.

Job location also can affect the kind of day care parents choose. Those who work in a business district and want to spend travel time with their children will be more likely to find day-care centers near their offices. Those who want their children close to home in a familiar neighborhood probably will have more choices of family or in-home day care.

Parents rarely find the perfect arrangement for themselves or for their children. Even with full-time child care, many parents end up creating a patchwork of different kinds of arrangements to cover themselves in the event of overtime or sick days. Some parents have a backup caregiver on call for such emergencies. Some communities provide health centers where children with colds, the flu, or chicken pox can be cared for, or provide health-care workers who come to the parents' home. These services are usually subsidized by local businesses. More often, however, parents find they must give up their own sick time to stay home with ill children.

Meeting Children's Needs in Child Care

Children's child-care needs depend on their ages and their temperaments. The best and worst ages for children to begin child care are described in more detail in chapter 3. Very young babies need caregivers who will focus loving attention solely on them through smiling, talking, and responding. They do not necessarily benefit from the company of other babies, but they do need interesting objects to explore. In *The Working Parents' Guide to Child Care*, child psychologist Bryna Siegel-Gorelick, Ph.D., recommends in-home care, if possible, for the first year of life. In a day-care setting, infants should get very attentive care from a few familiar adults.

One- and two-year-olds, however, can flourish in the social yet homelike atmosphere of family day care. Although they still need one-on-one attention, they can play alongside their peers, imitate them, and learn from them. Because they are mobile, toddlers can get to the caregiver whenever they need her. There should be enough space for children this age to move around freely and safely and enough duplicate toys so that these novice sharers are not in constant battle with one another.

A day-care center may not offer enough direct adult attention for infants and toddlers, but it can be ideal for children aged 2½ or older who speak well enough to communicate their needs to an often busy caregiver or to other children. Very independent or active children might start even earlier. Three-, four-, and five-year-olds are obviously ready to enjoy social life and to learn how to cooperate. Centers also often provide more challenging activities and materials for these older children than do day-care homes.

A child's temperament is as important a factor to consider as his age when deciding on appropriate child care. Some children do better in a one-on-one situation with an adult, others do better in a group; some are more oriented toward toys, others are more drawn to people. Some children are comfortable only with children at the same level of development, though most enjoy switching roles as they play with a wide range of children—leading one, following another, teaching one, learning from another.

If a child loves being outdoors every day, parents should choose day care with good outdoor facilities. A very sensitive child who is easily overstimulated may do better in family day care. Children who are very active and hard to control often have the most trouble in day care because they give caregivers the most trouble. For such children, day-care centers are often best because they are likely to provide more opportunities to work off steam and more adults to share the stress. Day-care centers also tend to have fixed routines, which can be calming for a very active child.

The children who most concern center directors, according to Jo Ann Miller and Susan Weissman in *The Parents' Guide to Day Care*, are very shy, quiet children, whose needs may be overlooked in a crowd. Parents should alert caregivers, then visit the site to make sure that these children do not spend all their time alone and that they get some individual attention. If a child rarely joins group activities, center day care may not be the right choice.

Once parents decide on what kind of day care to use, they should make sure that the caregiver's child-rearing philosophy closely matches their own beliefs and accommodates their child's temperament. Some caregivers arrange structured programs; others who are more laissez-faire allow children the freedom to choose their own activities. Day-care centers, for instance, are more likely to offer educational instruction at an early age than are family–day-care providers, who usually care for children of different ages. When children start day care, parents should discuss their child's temperament with the caregivers and listen to the caregivers' perceptions of their child as time goes on.

The choice of day care must be made carefully so that the arrangement will last. Most experts believe that continuity of care is important, especially for very young children. Unfortunately, studies show that the turnover rate in the child-care field is extremely high, mainly because of the very low salaries. A study by the Child Care Employee Project in Oakland, California, reported that turnover is 42 percent; in some cities it is as high as 64 percent. Even parents who have in-home caregivers report high turnover rates.

To remedy this, the National Association for the Education of Young Children (NAEYC) recommends professionalizing child care by introducing education and training requirements, enforced standards, and a higher wage scale. In France, for instance, caregivers in infant-toddler programs must have an education equivalent to two years of college in the United States and two more years of training in early childhood education and child development. Their salaries, reflecting this, are comparable to those of elementary school teachers and nurses. Partly as a result of these requirements, France has a much more stable child-care system than exists in the United States.

Choosing Child Care

Although it is important to understand the unique characteristics of each type of child care in making a choice, the setting is not the most important factor. In *The Preschool Years*, Ellen Galinsky and Dr. Judy David write, "It is the everyday relationship between the teacher-caregiver and the child—the greeting in the morning, the comments made when the child has drawn a picture, the affection and respect demonstrated—that is the single most important determinant of quality."

Locating the right child-care arrangement takes time. Although it is usually not necessary to begin a search more than two months in advance, it is a good idea to lay the groundwork as much as six months earlier. A few telephone calls can uncover what kinds of child care are available locally so that parents can make realistic plans.

Traditionally parents have found caregivers and day-care centers through community organizations, state and local agencies, pediatricians, the *Yellow Pages*, advertising, or word of mouth. More and more, though, they are turning to local resource and referral agencies. These agencies, which scout their area for the full range of child-care services, provide listings and counseling on how to make a choice, sometimes for a small fee. If none are listed in the telephone directory, parents can contact the National Association of Child Care Resource and Referral Agencies (2116 Campus Drive S.E., Rochester, MN 55904; (507) 287-2020).

In-Home Caregivers

The greatest advantage of in-home caregivers for babies and toddlers is that they are able to provide individual direct attention in a familiar environment. Older children cared for at home also are able to invite friends over to play, which isn't possible with center and family day care. In fact, this sort of play arrangement should be encouraged by in-home caregivers so that children don't miss the benefits and joys of playing with their peers. One mother helped her baby-sitter organize a baby-sitter–run play group that moved from house to house, modeled after the mother-run play group she had belonged to before she returned to work.

For parents, an in-home caregiver often can accommodate long working hours and overnight travel. When children are sick, someone will be home to care for them. (Of course, if the caregiver is sick, a substitute has to be found.) Parents also have the most control over an in-home caregiver because they set the rules. On the other hand, there is no supervisor, as in a day-care center, to enforce these rules.

When selecting an in-home caregiver, parents need to find one who shares their child-rearing values. Differences in style do not confuse a child, but differences in basic values do. A child can understand that Mommy tolerates a lot of commotion but that when Grandma is around he has to be quieter. In fact, he learns from this that people are different and react to him differently. It would be disturbing, however, if Grandma enforces the children-should-be-seen-but-not-heard rule all day long, while his parents encouraged him to share his feelings and opinions.

Many in-home caregivers are family members. This offers several obvious advantages. They know the parents and their ways, and they probably love the child and have a special interest in his development that someone who is not related would not have. Relatives also often do not charge for their services. Some parents feel, however, that unless they can find some way to repay a relative or do a favor in exchange, they cannot ask for what they want. Parents also should not assume that every relative shares their philosophy of child rearing. If Grandma, for example, raised her children differently—and better, as far as she is concerned— no one is going to change her ideas now. Battling over these issues can only strain family ties and stress a child.

Experts recommend that parents who want to hire a paid caregiver talk to many candidates on the telephone before making a choice, interview at least three, and carefully check references. Then, if the first candidates are unsuitable, the process should be repeated. Children should also meet any serious prospects so that parents can see how well they interact.

The interview can cover substantive issues, such as toilet training, biting, and discipline, but the questions should be neutral and open-ended (''How do you handle toilet training?'' ''What do you like to do with children?''). Parents should try not to state their own ideas on child rearing until they hear the caregiver's. Hypothetical questions (''What would you do if my two children were screaming and hitting each other?'') are often revealing. If housekeeping duties are part of the job, parents may want to stress that child care is the top priority and give an example (''If the laundry doesn't get done because you took the kids on a long trip to the zoo,'' a mother might say, ''I will be delighted''). But words are not enough. Parents should spend some time with the children and a new caregiver so that the caregiver can watch Mom singing silly songs to her three-year-old in the tub, or Dad jollying him through a meal or sending him to his room for a time-out.

Parents will still have to observe the relationship over time. Conversations are a good sign. If the caregiver talks to her charge and not at him, she is thinking of him as a person. Another good sign is a smooth transition when the first parent arrives home: a child who is alert and busy when the door opens and maintains that attitude in the presence of his parents. A child who demands constant stimulation from the moment his parents come home, however, may have spent too much time in front of the television set.

Day-care centers and some family–day-care providers ask parents to sign a contract so that the obligations and expectations of both parties are clear. Putting the agreement in writing in a less formal way is often helpful for in-home caregivers as well.

Family Day Care

Family day care takes place in the home of the provider. It is closer to a home situation than a day-care center, because ideally there are fewer other children and more individual attention. Parents should choose a family–day-care provider who adheres to the ratio guidelines that child development experts agree are important: one adult for every three infants or toddlers. Children in good family day care get the one-on-one contact they need for language development and the peer play they need for socialization by the end of the first year.

Most states limit the size of day-care homes to five or six children with a maximum of two infants, including the caregiver's own. Children may be of mixed ages, but it is best if younger children who are there full-time are no more than two years apart.

About half of family–day-care providers are women whose own children are grown and who see this as a rewarding way to earn some money at home. Many others become day-care providers in order to be able to stay home with their own young children. But they do not see their work as a career.

For parents with complicated schedules, some family–day-care providers offer somewhat flexible hours. The best ones also offer close contact and the feeling of an extended family for both parent and child.

As with in-home caregivers, parents must oversee their child's care themselves. They should visit at least three to five homes before making a decision and have at least two interviews at their favorite, with and without the child. The first interview can cover the practicalities of the arrangement, such as cost and hours. In the second, parents should try to find out if the caregiver shares their views on child rearing and get an idea of how the child would spend his time ("What kinds of things do you do with children?" "How might my child spend a typical day?"). Again, open-ended questions of the "How would you handle . . . ?" kind are best. The specific answers may be less telling than how intelligently and thoughtfully they are given. Parents will want to be assured that the caregiver isn't busy doing her chores all day, leaving the children to look after themselves or to do nothing but watch television. When she does chores, she should be willing to find ways to include the children to make it a learning experience. With a mother-caregiver, another concern is also how evenhandedly she handles problems between her children and the others in her care. Finally, a good day-care home should provide both indoor and outdoor play space and plenty of toys and creative materials.

The majority of family–day-care providers are not licensed and therefore are not supervised by any state or federal agencies or required to meet any standards. However, some corporations along with state governments are sponsoring programs to encourage day-care providers to become licensed. In New York, for example, the Golub Corporation, in an effort to find space in qualified day-care homes for children of the company's employees, is sponsoring a lending library to provide books and toys to family–day-care providers. It also offers free training for providers and help in applying for licensing that will give them access to financial benefits from the federal government.

If a day-care provider is not licensed, parents must determine to their own satisfaction that he or she has the equipment and services that satisfy basic children's safety and health needs, including clean floors and tables, heat covers on radiators, childproof safety seals on all electrical outlets, sturdy toys and play equipment, an outside play area that is free from hazards, childproof gates on stairs, first-aid supplies (in case a child scrapes himself while playing or becomes ill), nutritionally balanced meals and snacks, and healthy practices, such as hand washing between diaper changes.

The National Day Care Home Study, as part of the National Day Care Study, conducted by the government in the mid-1970s found that licensing made little difference in the quality of care. Quality was somewhat higher, however, in homes that belong to a family–day-care network. These networks, run by various community agencies such as YWCAs, colleges, or religious organizations, offer consultation to the providers and encourage professionalism. Parents should ask prospective family–day-care providers if they are members of a network or encourage them to join one.

Day-Care Centers

Day-care centers handle children from infancy through school age, though most start at age two and end when children begin school. They range in size from 20 to 200 children, but most have between 40 and 100. Most private day-care centers are run by churches, community organizations, and parent cooperatives. About 10 percent are subsidized by the government for low-income families and may offer other kinds of social support as well. There are also day-care–center chains run for profit. Some experts warn, however, that these centers may have to scrimp on staff salaries or materials in order to keep their fees affordable.

A good preschool day-care program offers the same kind of materials, experiences, and instruction as a good nursery school, but for a full day. There is usually more emphasis on education than in family day care, and children more often are placed with others of the same age. Although few states have formal requirements for education and training, caregivers at day-care centers are also more likely to have studied child development—one of the most important ingredients of quality child care, according to the National Day Care Study. In addition, caregivers at centers usually have no responsibilities other than child care.

In 1980 the government proposed optimal ratios of children to caregivers in day care. These Federal Interagency Day Care Requirements were never enacted, but they provide a high standard by which to judge programs. For infants and toddlers (up to age two), the child-to-caregiver ratio is 3:1; for ages two to three, 4:1; for ages three to six, 8:1. Even more important than these ratios, the researchers found, was the total size of the group. The maximum group size recommended for infants and toddlers is 6; for ages two to three, 12; and for ages three to six, 16. Many experts also recommend a separate room for babies, in part because infants do not yet have the immunities older children possess.

Parents considering a day-care center should visit at least twice, once with their child. They should ask the director about the philosophy and goals of the program, and then watch how these are achieved. Here are some questions to consider:

- Is the caregiving style permissive, authoritative, or authoritarian?
- How does the caregiving style relate to the parents' beliefs?
- Is there a balance between structure and openness?
- Is there a concern for children's safety?
- Is there a concern for their physical, emotional, and intellectual development?
- Does the center encourage parent involvement?
- What education and training do staff members have?
- Are the facilities clean?
- Do the children look happy and well cared for?

Dr. Bryna Siegel-Gorelick recommends to parents two methods for observing a day-care center effectively: Parents should first pick one youngster to follow—ideally one who reminds them of their own child; then they should watch the teacher-caregivers one at a time, noticing whether they work calmly and attentively with the children and cooperate and communicate with one another.

As the parents follow the child or the caregiver, they should observe how certain kinds of situations or activities are handled (fights over toys, mealtimes, departures). Transitions from one activity to the next should be smooth, and children should move through the day in small groups. Caregivers should be able to manage all the children at meals and other busy times and still meet individual needs.

For instance, not all of the children should be doing the same activity at the same time. There also should be a balance between whole-group, small-group, and individual activities.

Although most day-care centers are licensed, thus assuring certain minimal standards, the National Association for the Education of Young Children (NAEYC) accredits high-quality programs that apply. Parents can write to the NAEYC (1834 Connecticut Avenue N.W., Washington, DC 20009) for a complete listing in each state. Unfortunately, the number of high-quality day-care centers today is limited, and for those there may be long waiting lists. Middle-income parents may also find that the fees are too expensive for them to afford but that their income is too high for them to qualify for government assistance. Parents are urged nevertheless to put as much time and money as possible into finding and keeping quality day care, for it can make a demonstrable difference in a child's development.

Although many parents worry about it, child sexual abuse is actually relatively rare in day care (1 to 1.5 percent of all reported child abuse cases, according to the American Humane Association in 1985). Nevertheless, parents should be vigilant. Experts encourage parents to ask the directors of day-care centers how they handle behavior problems and to distrust any center that does not allow unannounced visits. Parents should look for signs of abuse in their child, including serious bruises or cuts, a change in personality or behavior, the mention of a secret, and a heightened interest in anything sexual.

Whatever kind of care parents choose for their child, they should reevaluate it after the first month and then check periodically that everything is going well. When they can, parents should get to know other parents whose children use the program and share and discuss with them any information or concerns they may have. This will help parents make sure their needs and their child's needs are being met. It can also help in lobbying for changes, such as the hiring of an added staff member for babies, the removal of an unqualified worker, or the establishment of a full-day program for school-age children during school vacations.

Parents' Feelings/Children's Feelings

In his book *Working and Caring,* Dr. T. Berry Brazelton points out that parents should prepare to grieve when they return to work. They will miss the intimacy they had with their babies, he writes, and the chance to watch them grow so closely. He adds that parents also feel "guilty, inadequate, helpless, hopeless, and even angry." They often worry about the long-term effects of substitute child care on their children.

Ideally parents' anxiety will drive them to find child care of the highest quality. They may, however, try to protect themselves from these feelings with one or more of three psychological defenses that Dr. Brazelton describes: Some parents may deny that the new child-care experience is important either to them or to their child. Some may feel so excluded from their child's experience that they become detached. ("Staying in touch and participating in your child's day care is the hardest job of all . . . " according to Dr. Brazelton, "because you care so deeply.") Finally, some may see the caregiver as the good parent and themselves as the bad, or the reverse. For example, one mother might interpret her two-year-old's perfectly normal tantrum as a sign of her failure as a mother. Another mother might criticize and try to control her caregiver because of feelings of competitiveness. Often parents resent the affection their children feel for their caregivers, when actually they should be pleased. These emotional conflicts are normal and common. Parents may find it helpful to talk about their feelings with each other, with friends, and with other parents.

What children worry about when their parents return to work is being left alone in an unfamiliar place or with unfamiliar people or both. To ease the transition to substitute care, experts recommend trying to arrange no other changes in the child's life while he is making this major adjustment. Parents should allow a week or two, if possible, for them and their child to adjust to the day-care situation before they actually start work. With an in-home caregiver, a parent should stay home the first day and then gradually leave for longer and longer stretches of time. If the child will be attending a center or day-care home, he should be taken for a visit before he starts so that he can meet the caregivers in his parents' presence. He may want to bring along a comforting object to remind him of home, and he may need to ease gradually into the routine. Parents should look for signs indicating that their child is doing well or for signs of stress that show difficulty in adjusting, such as nervousness about going to day care, sleeplessness, or clinginess. They may need to spend more one-on-one time with the child to help him make the transition.

Before day care begins, it is helpful to establish morning and evening routines and, if the child is old enough, tell him what will happen during the day. It also helps children to connect the parental pickup time with an event (''Daddy will be coming for you right after storytime''). Parents should try to anticipate concerns their child might have (''If you need a toy or to use the bathroom, you can tell Suzanne. She will help you'').

For many parents, drop-offs and pickups are heart-rending. However, there are ways to make them easier. A University of Miami study of two- to four-year-olds identified four techniques parents use that are likely to produce protest and tears: hovering around rather than leaving immediately, distracting the child from the reality of the departure, giving overlong explanations, and sneaking away. Instead, parents should help their child say good-bye by establishing a ritual: 10 kisses and a hug, for instance, or a wave from the window when parents are outside.

Parents should try to be on time for the pickup and greet their child enthusiastically. If possible, they should let him finish what he is doing or allow him to show them something exciting. And when they arrive home, parents should create the soothing and undemanding atmosphere that most children need after a busy, stimulating day, and give their child the exclusive attention that he probably will want.

On the weekends, parents should try to plan experiences for the child that will complement what he has been doing all week. If he is at home with a caregiver, he may want to be with other children. If he is in day care, he may want some one-on-one time. This time need be no more elaborate than following Mom around the house as she does her chores. She can explain to him what she is doing and find ways for him to help.

Children's adjustment to child care can take a few days or a few weeks, but usually by the tenth day they are at least used to it. Nevertheless, parents should expect and tolerate in their child some regression to more infantile behaviors: wetting his pants, sucking his thumb, using baby talk. And they should remember that their own relaxed attitude will ease their child's adjustment.

The Caregiver's Feelings

Caregivers are the most important element in any kind of child-care situation. Accordingly, parents should strive to make their relationship with the caregiver a happy and successful one. It is essential to treat caregivers with the respect due a professional. After all, parents and caregivers share an awesome responsibility. The caregiver should be made a partner in handling the child's problems and be allowed to enjoy the child's successes. And a schedule of regular talks between parents and caregivers will allow both sides the opportunity to discuss problems before they escalate.

In a career pamphlet entitled *Nanny*, Nicole Exantus states frankly, "Many employers don't take the job very seriously. It's a pity that they don't realize what a job it is. And it's a two-way street. If you look at a nanny as just someone you pay to get things done, then that's what she's going to give you back. And who's going to suffer but that little person."

Self-Care

Children in self-care is the current euphemism for what are otherwise called latchkey children. According to recent surveys, there are between 2 and 6 million children under the age of 13 (the majority of whom are middle class) who regularly take care of themselves after school and on weekends. In third world countries, this is not unusual. In fact, children as young as eight are often put in charge of younger siblings when their parents are away. These children, however, are not isolated behind the locked doors of a house or an apartment; rather, they are within easy reach of familiar adults in their extended family.

Although parents tend to worry most about their children's physical safety, the real problems for most children are fear and boredom. In *The Working Parent Dilemma*, Rabbi Earl Grollman and Gerri Sweder reported that when they had asked 641 children across the country to finish a story about how it would feel to be alone at home each day, the most universal response was a description of loneliness. Many children also said they would be scared and would worry about noises or someone breaking in. In addition, a recent study by the universities of Southern California and Illinois found that eighth graders who were at home alone more than 11 hours a week were twice as likely to use tobacco, alcohol, and marijuana than were those who were supervised by adults.

Most experts do not believe children are developmentally ready to be alone before the age of 10 or 12, and even then, this should not happen routinely for long periods of time. Younger children do not even have the decision-making skills to handle problems.

Some communities have started after-school programs for school-age children where they can play safely with others. Unfortunately, there are not enough of these and many are expensive. Transportation back and forth can also be a problem. Programs in the child's own school may end before 5 p.m., too early for working parents. In some communities, the children's book section in the public library has become a popular after-school haunt for latchkey children. Most librarians, however, are not prepared to supervise these children and resent the added responsibility.

Parents who leave their children alone should prepare them for unforeseen circumstances. Whenever a child is home alone he should be given the same emergency information as a baby-sitter. Parents should discuss safety rules and reinforce them by asking hypothetical questions ("What would you do if someone rang the bell and asked to come in and use the telephone?"). They should also locate and introduce to the child at least two adults who would be available to help in an emergency.

As soon as the child arrives home, he should call a parent or another familiar adult. This routine gives parents peace of mind and provides the child with a comfortable transition from a social to a solitary environment. Many children are also less lonely when they come home to a pet, a turned-on light, or a playing radio, or when they have permission to visit friends. They will be less bored if they have planned a schedule of pleasurable, productive activities to do so that they do not just sit in front of the television for hours. These might include taking part in community recreation or volunteer activities once a week or an ongoing project that can be worked on when they come home. Finally, parents should arrive home when they promise, even if they have to put off errands. Children worry about parents who are late as much as parents worry about tardy children.

There are some children who flourish alone after school, but they are in the minority. In most cases, especially for children under 13, self-care is an arrangement that suits the needs of the parents at the expense of the needs of the child. Parents should encourage a child of any age who is in self-care to talk about his feelings and fears. According to Dr. Jay Belsky, a child who has a good relationship with his parents will be better able to handle being alone.

The Future

As more and more women with young children enter the work force and child care becomes a more pressing issue, parents are becoming more insistent in their demands to government and industry for help in meeting their needs. For the sake of America's children, these sectors will have to respond soon with financial assistance and enforced regulations to improve the quality of child care. Meanwhile, parents can be a powerful force in providing the best for their children by speaking out about what they need and by joining forces with other parents in planning and evaluating what is available.

CHAPTER FIVE

• • • • • •

New Roles for Parents: Divorced, Single, and Step-

My husband and I separated when my daughter was 3½, but I was really a single parent from the day she was conceived. My husband loves her in his way, but he's never taken any responsibility for her, not even financial.

At first I felt inadequate, totally overwhelmed, alone, frustrated, panicked. I had nightmares that I wasn't doing the right thing, that I was going to ruin everything by saying no to my daughter. I used to feel guilty for not giving her the two-parent family I had.

Every day is still a struggle. There is always this ongoing weariness. As a single parent, you're always on. It must be really nice to come home and say to your husband, "What should we do about this?" Or to have a point in the day to look forward to when Dad will walk in the door and take some of the heat off.

Jenny was brought up on two words: flexibility and co-operation. She has a different kind of responsibility than her friends do. She is very cognizant of the fact that we pay for things, that I'm working very hard for us. I don't want her to feel guilty, and I wish she didn't have to worry about money, but I demand that she respect what I do for us. I want my daughter to have character. When she gets out of here she'll be able to survive.

—A SINGLE MOTHER

I separated from my wife and left the house when my daughter, Emma, was two. I moved to another city for a job, expecting that she and her mother might follow if we were able to reconstruct our marriage. That didn't work, but I made an enormous effort to keep in contact with my daughter. I went back every other weekend, and I made my telephone billing number accessible to her so that it would never be an issue if she wanted to call me. I talked to her almost every day for at least a couple of minutes. That happens to this day, and she is almost nine now. I have a very close relationship with her.

When Emma was about six, her mother remarried and I met the person whom I later married. Now I have a stepson, Peter, who is about nine months older than my daughter. Peter's father left when he was three months old. He lives nearby, but sometimes he won't call Peter for two or three months at a time.

Peter and I hit it off very early, but he was terribly afraid of being abandoned again. And one thing that's come up recently indicates that there's still turbulence. If I get on him about something he's done, instead of getting angry at me and saying, ''You're being mean!'' his anger comes back at himself and he'll say, ''I'm just an awful person.'' I'm not a real father whom he can risk getting furious at.

It took a lot of work putting the family together, especially since Emma only comes here for weekends once a month now. Peter had a tremendously difficult time with her arrivals because he knew how passionately I felt about her. And she was terribly jealous that he was with me all the time. To this day she has a fantasy that her mother and I will get back together.

Soon after we got married, my wife informed me, ''Do you notice that you're very hard on Peter about his behavior and Emma just doesn't get called on hers?'' I was amazed.

I had been behaving that way since she was two, and it was fueled by an enormous amount of guilt. But I saw the importance of being evenhanded with them and assuring both kids that they were loved.

I say that I consider Peter as much my son as if I had been his natural father. I'd leap into icy water to rescue either kid—but there's a difference. And I'm not quite at peace with what that difference is.

—A FATHER AND STEPFATHER

I met Tom's children when Maggie was six and Timothy was nine. Tom was just in the final stages of his divorce, and he had the kids every other weekend. The minute we met, Timothy wanted to be my best friend, but Maggie was very reserved. I think Timothy sized up the situation, saw that his father loved me, and figured that the only way to be happy was to love me, too. But his true feelings were masked. When he became rebellious during high school, he saw me as a selfish, hedonistic woman who only wanted his father. When the fights started, it was, "You're not my mother! You can't tell me what to do!"

Because Maggie was younger, it was easier for her to allow me to tell her what to do, to take care of her. She also could talk more about her feelings than Timothy did, and that made it easier. When we first met, she asked me, "Are you going to have a baby some day?" I said, "I'd like to." And she said, "I'm not worried because by then my mother and father will be back together." She also would tell me how much better than me her mother was.

Meanwhile, their mother was still so angry at Tom that she used to say terrible things about him to the kids. But we would never say anything bad about her. We would just say, "Some of the things your mother says don't make sense, but she's a good person."

After about two years, their mother had a nervous break-down and the kids came to live with us. I was very idealistic. I loved kids, and I wanted a family. Tom didn't want more children at that time, so this was my instant family. But it was a different kind of family. It took me a while to own them, and then only with some ambivalence. They already had a mother. And while I was trying to love them, I was also resenting them because in my mind they were interfering with my having children. But I can honestly say now, after so many years, that I love them very much.

Now that Tim and Maggie are older [25 and 22], you would think that our having children would be okay. But, in fact, they're both having a hard time. I've talked to them about it and I've said many times that my having children is not to replace them, but to add to our family. Whether they believe it, I don't know.

For me, the worst part of being a stepparent is facing the fact that they're not your children. They're only loaned to you for a few years and you never know how they will feel about you when they grow up. I sometimes wonder if their relationship with their mother will become stronger and stronger as the years go by. I sometimes think: What would happen if their father died? What if I put in all that time and they didn't love me when they got older?

—A MOTHER AND STEPMOTHER

One of the greatest changes the American family has faced in the last 30 years is the dramatic rise in divorce. In the early 1960s the divorce rate was 20 to 25 percent of married couples. Now it is estimated that 48 percent of marriages will end in divorce, affecting 40 percent of today's children. In addition, about 25 percent of children today will live with a stepparent before they reach the age of 16. In 1985, according to the U.S. Census Bureau, the number of stepchildren under 18 was almost 6.8 million.

Even children who do not experience divorce in their immediate families usually know a relative or friend who has.

The prevalence of divorce and remarriage has stretched the definitions of "parent" and "family." Many mothers and fathers today face the challenge of the new and often baffling roles (sometimes in combination) of single parent, custodial parent, noncustodial parent, joint-custodial parent, and stepparent. Children may find their families expanding in confusing ways as stepparents and step-relatives are added to both sides.

Though today parents from traditional families can still look to their own parents for a core of social and family values, they do not provide adequate models for lives of separation and recombination. There are no precedents to show men how to be fathers to their children every other weekend and for six weeks in the summer. There is no easy answer to the question of how to apply the commandment "Honor thy father and thy mother" to stepparents. Holiday traditions also often have to be reshaped to accommodate new family forms: Christmas Eve and Christmas Day may become two different holidays; birthdays are often celebrated twice. And, unfortunately, social norms that have not yet coped with names for new kinds of kin (is a stepfather's father a "grandfather"?) cannot possibly settle issues of affection and authority.

Meanwhile, parents who were encouraged by experts in the 1970s and early 1980s to believe that divorce was a perfect cure for everyone in an unhappy marriage are now being warned by today's experts that they may have permanently harmed their children. In their recent book *Second Chances*, based on a long-term study of divorced families, psychologist Judith S. Wallerstein, Ph.D., and journalist Sandra Blakeslee reported that five years after a parental divorce only 34 percent of the children were doing well, and after 10 years the number had reached only

45 percent. Almost half entered adulthood "worried, underachieving, self-deprecating, and sometimes angry."

Critics of Dr. Wallerstein's work, however, point to flaws in the study, including the small, unrepresentative sample and the absence of a control group, and claim that the long-term effects of divorce are much exaggerated. They also cite contradictory evidence. The 1981 National Survey of Children, for instance, found only modest differences in the well-being of adolescents from divorced or separated families and those from intact families.

Even Dr. Wallerstein does not recommend staying married "for the sake of the children." "All our evidence," she concludes, "shows that children turn out less well adjusted when exposed to open conflict, where parents terrorize or strike one another, than do children from divorced families. And . . . it is not useful to provide children with a model of adult behavior that avoids problem solving and that stresses martyrdom, violence, or apathy. A divorce undertaken thoughtfully and realistically can teach children how to confront serious life problems with compassion, wisdom, and appropriate action."

Fortunately, as divorce has become more common, experts have begun to identify some of the ways in which parents can make it easier for their children.

Parenting Through Divorce

For children, a divorce begins when their parents announce it, and it is almost always a shock no matter how old the children are or how accustomed they are to parental conflict. As painful as family life may have been, it is all that they know, and they expect it to continue forever. What to tell children about an impending divorce depends on their age and how much they can understand. But all children need to be assured—more than once and by both mother and father—that their parents' love for them will remain constant and that the divorce is in no way their fault, nor can they do anything to change it. Children also need to know exactly how their daily lives will be affected: where they will live, where the parent who is moving out will live, and when they will see him or her.

Children also should be given truthful answers to the inevitable question, "Why?", tailored to their age and ability to understand. ("Daddy and I are no longer happy living together," a mother might say to a nine-year-old. "We fight all the time.") Parents' answers should not include negative comments about each other or upsetting details. If one parent is suffering from alcohol or drug abuse, for example, a child could be told simply that the parent is not well and needs special help.

Glossing over the experience with a "Pretty soon we're all going to be happier than ever!" is unrealistic and can be damaging. By explaining that healing takes time, parents can help children avoid feelings of failure or betrayal when they do not bounce back instantly. Sharing sadness also gives children the freedom to express their own feelings and helps them better understand their parents' emotional ups and downs.

In his book *Growing Up with Divorce*, Neil Kalter, Ph.D., director of the Center for the Child and Family at the University of Michigan, describes some aspects of children's development that affect how they may respond to the divorce process at different ages. Infants and toddlers, for instance, are distressed when they are separated from their primary caregiver. They also have trouble sustaining intense relationships with people whom they do not see often. For them, short, frequent visits with the absent parent may be better than longer but less frequent ones.

Preschoolers and children under eight years old tend to see themselves as the cause of everything that happens and may blame themselves for the divorce. They confuse what is real with what is imaginary and may have frightening fantasies, worrying perhaps that both parents will abandon them or that they will hurt each other. Parents can reassure them by providing a consistent schedule and as much one-on-one time as possible, and by being patient with fears, real or imagined.

Older elementary school children, according to Dr. Kalter, often suffer painful internal conflicts. They may feel both love and anger toward their parents, for instance, or loyalty to each but with an impulse to take sides. The natural desire to be with their own friends often conflicts with a wish to comfort a needy or lonely parent. Children this age may also protect themselves from their emotions in subtle and misleading ways. A child may act bossy when she is actually frightened, or indifferent when she wants to avoid painful feelings. Parents who are aware of the stressful conflicts that may underlie their children's behavior can be careful not to inflame the conflicts. For instance, they can resist using children as allies or spies against the other parent, or depending on them too greatly for emotional or practical support. Children this age also need more than words of love from their parents. They need concrete proof of their commitment in time spent together and in shared activities.

Teenagers, who feel many of the same conflicts as younger children, bear the additional stress of the developmental challenges for their age. They are testing their independence but need more than ever a secure home base to which they can return. Because of teens' abilities, however, parents may lean heavily on them and may slack up on guidance and discipline. Adolescents need parental role models to help them establish their own identities. They tend to have a rigid sense of right and wrong, however, and may judge their divorcing parents harshly. Because of their own sexual tensions, they may be particularly upset by their parents' dating. Teenagers may keep their feelings to themselves or turn their anger or sadness into actions such as drinking or reckless driving, which can be dangerous to themselves and others. Experts encourage divorcing parents to continue providing a firm structure for their teenagers and to keep trying to communicate with them, while respecting their need for autonomy. The divorce experience can also be made easier for adolescents if it does not create dramatic changes in their lives, such as a move to a new school.

All children experiencing a parental divorce may regress in their behavior and temporarily act less maturely. They may be angry and fearful; have extreme mood swings; complain of stomachaches and headaches; become anxious, sad, or withdrawn; or misbehave at school or at home. If these signs of distress are very intense, last for a long time, or interfere with their child's development, it is wise for parents to consult a mental health professional.

Most experts agree that a child's adjustment to divorce is closely tied to the emotional well-being of the custodial parent (the mother in 90 percent of divorces). For many custodial parents, divorce results in a triple whammy: coping with the emotionally debilitating combination of sadness, loneliness, anger, and battered self-esteem; the physical stress of usually having to do a two-person job alone; and the financial pressure of living on a sharply reduced income. Most divorced fathers take their earning power with them; few pay adequate child support. According to a national survey, the Panel Study of Income Dynamics, in the year following legal marital separation, the standard of living for mothers and children falls by about one third.

These problems can distract parents from seeing their children's needs and can drain them of time and energy. Especially during the first year after divorce, parents may be preoccupied, communicate poorly, and act less affectionately. Financial need may force them to spend more hours at work and away from the children. Both parents may discipline inconsistently, giving in to demands because of guilt, fear of rejection, or just plain fatigue. Some children, too, try to take advantage of parental conflict and competition, angling for material possessions and extra privileges. Yet all children, from preschoolers through adolescents, need a solid base at home—firm rules, routines, and expectations—in order to venture confidently into the world.

According to Dr. Kalter, communication is the "cornerstone of assisting all children faced with crisis." He encourages parents to use puppets, dolls, action figures, drawings, and stories to act out any signs of unhappiness they may see in their young children. By these indirect means they can encourage their children to express their feelings about the divorce, and offer ways to help them cope.

With older children, Dr. Kalter recommends that parents try an indirect approach, for example, talking about "some kids," "some guys," or "some girls" ("Some kids feel angry all the time when their parents get divorced and sometimes get into fights at school even though they don't really want to"). This method may also work with adolescents; however, children that age usually want and need to be talked to directly as well.

A common by-product of divorce that is most painful to children is the continuing hostility between their parents. According to Dr. Kalter, these feelings of anguish and fury "resonate" most intensely in very young children, causing them great stress because their emotions are not yet completely independent of those of their parents. In addition, older children may feel torn in their allegiances.

Thus, divorcing parents should strive to communicate and cooperate with each other rather than to let their feelings rule or to compete for their children's affection. If their rage is too great to restrain in front of the children, parents may need to minimize their contact, perhaps by limiting to writing their communications about anything other than scheduling. They might also need help from a mental health professional in order to proceed with their own lives.

The Noncustodial Parent

Losing a relationship with the noncustodial parent (usually the father) is another by-product of divorce that is extremely upsetting for children. As a result, children (such as Peter in the story at the beginning of this chapter) may suffer persistent, deep feelings of rejection. In her book *Vicki Lansky's Divorce Book for Parents,* Lansky advises custodial parents to allow the absent parent frequent visits, if possible, and to ease children's loneliness between times by encouraging contact with grandparents and other close adults.

In divorce, the absence of the father is frighteningly common. In a study of children from disrupted families from 1976 to 1987, University of Pennsylvania sociologists Frank F. Furstenburg, Jr., Ph.D., and Kathleen Harris, Ph.D., found that more than half of those children with noncustodial fathers had never been in their fathers' homes; 42 percent had not even seen them during the past year. Only one in six saw the father on an average of once a week or more.

Yet not all of these men are selfish and indifferent. Noncustodial parents face a difficult and depressing adjustment to a new, reduced parental role. They often live with an abiding sense of loss. In place of daily interaction with their children, they often are allotted short, scheduled visits, which may seem awkward and superficial. Some have former spouses who continue to wage the divorce war using visitation as their weapon.

The role of noncustodial parents also has no clear definition. What rights and responsibilities do they have? Are they allowed to pass judgment on their children's behavior? Are they allowed to discipline them? Can they even afford to do so without fear of losing them? Feeling cut off from their children's lives and doubting that they will have any lasting influence on them, these parents may drop out in despair. A psychiatric social worker quoted by Stephen L. Atlas in *The Official Parents Without Partners Sourcebook* explains that it can take several months or years for people to realize that they can still be parents even if they don't live with their children full-time. ''Parenthood is your relationship to your children,'' she writes; ''custody is where the children live. In my noncustodial single-parent workshop, I ask my students to define 'parent' and ask how many [parenting] qualities they feel still apply. Some of their definitions include caretaker, disciplinarian, caring person, nurturer, provider, and assumer of responsibility.''

There are a number of ways in which noncustodial parents can make the visiting situation feel more normal and be more meaningful for themselves and their children. Most important, children should not be treated as guests in the noncustodial home. They should have rules and responsibilities, and there should be a special place to keep their belongings. To enter the flow of their children's everyday life, noncustodial parents can make an effort to participate in some of their after-school activities, whether it be to coach them in soccer or to shuttle them to dentist appointments. Parents can also encourage children to bring their homework or invite a friend when they visit.

The nature of the visit should also suit the age of

the child. Toddlers may be happier sometimes with noncustodial-parent visits in their own homes. Older children may resent visiting if it interferes with their social lives and may appreciate a more flexible schedule. If there are several children, the noncustodial parent needs to find some private time to be with each, if only for a few minutes during the visit. And occasionally separate visits can be arranged.

Joint Custody

Recently the concept of joint custody has aroused hope as a possible solution to two of the problems of divorce: the loss of one parent and the overload of the other. Children in joint custody have a separate home with each parent, where they spend a significant amount of time, usually during part of each week or alternate weeks. Although this arrangement is still relatively uncommon, it has been accepted in 41 states and is the presumption or preference in more than 13.

Joint custody is not a cure-all. In order for it to work, parents need to live close to each other. They need to be able to create some common rules for their children and to accept each other's different parenting styles and lifestyles. Hardest of all, they need to be able to communicate regularly without blowing up at each other. Children must be able to pack up and move frequently without too much distress and adapt to the differences between homes.

Joint custody is often more difficult with infants and toddlers, who need a consistent environment. Dr. Kalter suggests that both homes be as alike as possible, with the same kinds of crib, blankets, and bottles, and that special familiar objects be brought back and forth. On days the children spend with one parent, they may still need a quick visit from the other. For very young children or for those with less easygoing temperaments, it may be too stressful to move back and forth between two homes. By the time children reach the age of six, separations are usually easier for them to deal with. The young elementary school child can move more comfortably between two houses because she has a better understanding of space and time. Adolescents, however, often prefer a single home—and telephone number.

Vicki Lansky recommends that parents with joint custody work to establish a routine that reflects their children's needs and desires as well as their own. She also suggests that the children be included in the planning. Although the schedule should be fixed, it should remain flexible enough so that a business trip or sleep-over won't create a major emergency. Lansky also recommends that parents help children keep a checklist of their belongings so that necessities do not get left behind during a move.

So far, there has been little research on how the experience of joint custody affects children over a long period of time. Dr. Wallerstein, who conducted the only reported study of young children in joint-custody arrangements, concluded that after two years children were "not necessarily protected from the deleterious affects of divorce simply because of joint custody. Nor is there any evidence that good joint custody better serves these children than good single custody when the noncustodial parents stay involved." On the other hand, she did find that fathers in families with joint custody were more committed to their children, though this may have been what led to the arrangement rather than its effect.

Because no one yet knows what difference, if any, joint custody makes in the long term, parents today have to judge for themselves what will most benefit them and their children. In general, though, the best arrangements for children are those that are the least stressful.

Flying on One Engine:
The Single-Parent Family

The vast majority of single parents are divorced women who have custody of their children. However, many single parents are young women who have never been married and often are also uneducated and poor. Others are "single mothers by choice," usually older and better prepared to be parents and providers. And still other single parents are widows and widowers. Finally, a small but growing number of single parents (about 2 percent of families with children under age 18) are fathers who have custody of their children. These men have taken the opportunity to become more nurturing and involved with their children than traditional fathers. Many also have the advantage of being better off financially than single mothers.

All single parents, however, have certain concerns in common. For most, discipline is the thorniest issue. After a long day at work and hours of housework ahead, single parents often simply do not have the energy to discipline their children. ("I'm always so tired, it's just easier to say yes than no," admitted one recently divorced mother.) Single parents may feel guilty that their children have suffered so much already or that they themselves no longer have time to balance discipline with enough expressions of love. Yet "seeing discipline as a form of giving is a developmental step for a parent," writes Dr. T. Berry Brazelton in *Working and Caring*.

Some single parents are relieved not to have to disagree with a spouse about child rearing, but, says one, "for the most part it's harder. You don't have anybody to back you up." In *The Woman Who Works, the Parent Who Cares*, Dr. Sirgay Sanger and John Kelly recommend invoking the

119

names of alternative authority figures, such as aunts, uncles, or grandparents, for support (''Uncle Ben would be really proud of you for working so hard on this project,'' or ''Grandma feels strongly, as I do, that you should go to religious school'').

By their nature, single-parent families are often more democratic than intact families. Because the children usually are expected to help out more, they also want a bigger voice in family decisions: what they eat and when, how chores are allocated, what kind of vacations will be taken, what the rules are for television watching. To make sure that everyone's ideas are considered, many families schedule regular meetings.

''The strength of the single-parent household lies in its shared recognition of interdependence,'' writes sociologist Robert S. Weiss, Ph.D., in *Going It Alone*. This recognition increases the chances that children will understand what needs to be done and will accept their responsibilities. It also promotes communication between parent and children and fosters a strong sense of family cooperation.

Even in the most democratic families, however, parents usually want to reserve the right of ultimate authority. They might discuss with a teenager, for instance, what would be an acceptable curfew and try to respond to any reasonable objections. But the final decision would be the parents'. And it is the rare parent who will negotiate at all about the use of drugs or other dangers to safety or health.

Experts warn that the close bond that often develops between single parents and their children—and that helps the family to run smoothly—can become too tight. Some single parents put their children in the unhealthy position of advisors or confidants. A boy may feel he must become the man of the house; a girl may become her father's hostess and housekeeper. These unnatural roles interfere with children's development and may make it harder for them to move out on their own, especially if they feel responsible for a parent's happiness.

In *Working and Caring,* Dr. Brazelton points out that single parents, especially single mothers by choice, are tempted sometimes to restrict their children too much. He advises them to find ways to help their children achieve the important developmental goals of separation and independence by encouraging their relationships with other adults including caregivers and, most especially, grandparents. Otherwise, some single parents may inadvertently stand in the way of their children's psychological growth. "This is one of the more difficult aspects of the single parent's relationship with a child," Dr. Brazelton writes.

All single parents need to find outside sources of support for themselves, too, wherever they can, whether from old friends or new; a support group; a therapist; or a job which, though demanding, may bolster self-esteem and also open up a new social world. One divorced mother, for instance, built a network of single office friends, whose social lives were more suited to fulfilling her present needs than were those of her married friends.

Taking good care of their own mental health will also assure single parents of the emotional strength needed to take good care of their children. "I know people who will not go out on a Saturday night because they have custody of their kids," noted a woman who dated a divorced father for three years before they got married. "I don't think that's good. In our case, we would spend all day with the kids, but at night we went out. If my husband hadn't gotten what he needed, I don't think he could have given the kids what they needed."

Stepping Into New Roles

For children of all ages, another great stress related to divorce is coping with the remarriage of their parents, especially of the custodial parent. They may fear the loss of a special relationship they have had with that parent, and they finally will have to abandon all hope of the family being reunited. Some children feel torn emotionally: disloyal to their natural parent if they begin to like the stepparent, and excluded from the new family if they keep their distance.

Experts claim that the younger children are, the more easily they adjust to remarriage. Very young children are more flexible and need the help that a second parent provides. Children who have the hardest time joining a stepfamily are usually those between the ages of nine and 15. Some of these older children will have taken on semi-adult roles as helper and comforter in the single-parent family and may resent having to give up their place and retreat to the position of being a child again. Adolescents, who are going through so many changes of their own, may be knocked off balance by a new situation at home, especially one that has sexual aspects. The adolescent's need to break away from the family also conflicts with the stepparent's need to unite it.

The most difficult step-relationships seem to be between stepmothers and stepdaughters. This may be because young girls identify strongly with their mothers and resist any replacement. They also may feel that they are competing for their father's affection.

The best course in introducing a new parent and building a stepfamily is to move gradually. Children and the prospective spouse should be given plenty of opportunities to get to know each other—with and without the natural parent present. Spending time together will build a core of shared memories and will help to make the transition into marriage easier.

Before remarrying, parents should discuss with their children any foreseeable changes, such as moving to a new house, living with step-siblings, and compromising on rules. An early decision should be made jointly about the names stepchildren and stepparents will call each other. The natural parent should try to include the children in some adult plans and also assure them that they will still have private times together without the stepparent.

Continuing communication among family members is crucial, especially in households with older children, who may be troubled by sexual issues. Parents and stepparents can help teenagers by encouraging them to discuss any feelings of fear, sadness, anger, or embarrassment that they may have.

Being a part of a stepfamily is stressful for adults, too. Society has not yet set guidelines concerning how the members of a stepfamily should relate to each other or to the other natural parent who exists outside the marriage. "What seems to work best for most stepfamilies," write Ellen Galinsky and Dr. Judy David in *The Preschool Years*, "is to see children as members of two family units. It is better if all members of the stepfamily accept and keep the boundaries open to both old and new family ties. Attempting to shut out these relationships is to deny reality." The stepparent can help to smooth the relationship between both family units by showing respect for the absent parent and for the love and loss the children feel. And even if the stepparent detests the absent parent, this feeling should not be allowed to pollute the relationship with the stepchildren.

Most stepparents feel ill-prepared for their role. It differs greatly from being a natural parent, the only model many have had. "It was much harder than I expected," said one stepmother. "There was that feeling of insecurity about what I was doing, as if I were on someone else's turf and had no real right to make a claim." Unrealistic expectations also can mar stepparents' satisfaction with their role. "It's a no-win situation," according to one stepmother. "I carted them around and listened to them. One hour every night for two years I worked with the youngest boy on his spelling. No way could I get back the same emotional response and commitment I gave them. You just do not get the same payback as a natural parent does."

Stepparents should see themselves not as replacements for the natural parent, but as additional parents. One stepfather described what he told his new teenage stepsons: "I never said to them 'I'm your father now and you have to deal with me.' I said, 'We're a family now.' "

Becoming friends is often the best initial goal for stepparents. In *Strengthening Your Stepfamily*, writer Elizabeth Einstein, and parent educator Linda Albert, write that "in the role of friend, a stepparent can provide additional caring and concern. Offering friendship is far less threatening than coming in to take over. When you build your role from the basis of friendship, you give children time to come to know and respect you."

Unfortunately, many stepparents have to contend with the myths that they should instantly love their stepchildren and that the children will instantly love them. The opposite is more often the case—especially at first, when new family members are trying to adjust to each other. Stepparents may be met with hostility and criticism and sometimes even attempts to sabotage the marriage from children whose behavior can be appalling. It's important that parents try not to take this personally, since after a divorce children often react negatively to aspects of their lives that have nothing to do with the stepparent.

After a time of living together, love may develop, but

stepparents shouldn't be disconsolate if it doesn't. One stepmother advised her husband not to ask his four-year-old son in her presence if he loved her. "I could see that he was faced with a terrible conflict of pleasing his father, not wanting to hurt my feelings, and not betraying his mother," she said. "By the time he was six, he understood that he could love many people for many different reasons. Then he felt comfortable saying 'I love you' to me in a heartfelt manner." On the other hand, in his book *Stepfathering*, Mark Bruce Rosin, M.A., points out that "because there is no single definition of what a stepfather should be, it is fallacious to assume that a stepfather who describes his role as 'like a father' is succeeding while a stepfather who describes his role as 'like an uncle' or 'like a friend' is failing."

Discipline is an area that many stepparents find difficult to handle, especially those who are trying to make a place for themselves in a well-established single-parent household. Most experts recommend that stepparents ease into the parental role gradually. They should work first to establish friendship, respect, and trust, so that the children will want to win their approval and will thus accept their discipline. Meanwhile, however, they should be careful not to let their stepchildren walk all over them.

In general, new families should work out the most important rules together in advance. At first the stepparent can let the natural parent do the enforcing, but the goal, most experts believe, is for both parents to play equal roles. If a child says, "You're not my father. You can't tell me what to do," a stepparent can answer, "That's right. I'm not your biological father. But I'm the adult responsible for you now, and I have to enforce the rules." Even the spouse of the noncustodial parent, who usually has a lesser role, should be able to require acceptable behavior in her own home.

Because stepparents do not necessarily act out of love and usually do not get a full "payback" for what they do from their stepchildren, they deserve at least a thank-you from their spouses. Stepparents also deserve some time and space to nurture their adult relationship. They may have entered the marriage with their eyes open, but they will still miss the privacy of a first marriage and have normal feelings of jealousy over sharing their spouse's time with the children.

Combined Families

When two families combine, there are even more possible sources of conflict and jealousy. Some experts recommend moving into a new "neutral" home, if possible, so that neither family feels that it has an edge or that it has been displaced. Even then, some children may resent having to share their parents and their household space with stepbrothers or stepsisters. Older children may have trouble adjusting suddenly to being the middle or youngest child in the new family. For others, especially those who were only children, the advantages of live-in playmates may offset any disadvantages.

The birth of a new baby in a stepfamily also affects children very differently. For some, the baby represents the final death of the original marriage. Some children fear that the baby will take their place in their parents' affections. A baby also can draw everyone closer together because they are all finally related through the new family member.

The degree of jealousy children feel in these circumstances is greatly influenced by how both parents treat them. All children in combined families should have the same privileges and responsibilities, depending on their ages. Their appearances, abilities, talents, or interests should never be compared. Parents should help them to find private spaces for their possessions and allow them private time to pursue their own interests.

Combined families also have to deal with the issues of sexual attraction in a situation where the incest taboo is unclear. In the course of first negotiating rules for the new family, standards of dress and undress should be set, along with bathroom and bedroom etiquette, to help children ensure their modesty and privacy while living with new family members who are strangers at first, or with step-siblings who may have been school- or playmates before. Parents should also encourage communication to help confront any confused sexual feelings.

Grandparents in combined families should be encouraged to form good relationships with their step-grandchildren while maintaining their relationships with their natural grandchildren. They can be asked to treat the children equally when giving gifts and to respect everyone's feelings, but parents cannot prevent them from favoring their natural grandchildren. They may need to be reminded, however, of how much their behavior and attitudes affect the whole family. And parents should listen to the grandparents' feelings, too.

Parents themselves cannot be expected to love their natural children and their stepchildren equally. It is possible for parents to be honest about their feelings while still acknowledging that their stepchildren are important to them. ''I do care about my children more right now,'' a stepparent might say, ''because I have known them all their lives, just as your parent has a special relationship with you. But I hope as we get to know each other better, we will keep growing closer and closer.''

The Silver Lining

Although the stresses inherent in remarriage are real, Dr. Kalter points out that it also offers "opportunities for enhanced emotional and social growth." Children who knew only an unhappy marriage are now able to observe a loving adult relationship as a future role model. Stepparents can help give their same-sex stepchildren a firm sense of masculine or feminine identity, while they can help opposite-sex children achieve more social self-confidence. Stepparents also can fill the role of mentor or confidant to children who want those relationships. Some experts have even suggested that children who cope with stressful life experiences, such as divorce and remarriage, may grow up to be more flexible and competent adults.

For the family, the divorce epidemic of the last few decades is probably the most fearsome attack it will ever have to face. Divorce batters and tears at the very structure of the institution. Perhaps the greatest testament to the family is that it seems to have been able to repel that attack by calling on its natural strengths: its flexibility and its dedication to the healthy development of children. Men and women have created new roles and redefined old ones. But this has not been accomplished without a price, to which anguished and exhausted single parents can attest. At the peak of the divorce crisis in this nation, families were left to cope mainly on their own. Only recently have social institutions begun to respond to the crying needs of the victims of divorce. Only recently could parents and children dare to hope for social support for such basic needs as good, affordable child care, enforced child-support payments, and creative custody arrangements. Even so, they must continue to make their voices heard by local and national governments.

PART III

······

Where Do We Go from Here?

"IT'S FIGHT DRUGS, FIGHT POLLUTION, AND FIGHT CHOLESTEROL, BUT FIGHT EDDIE WOOD, AND YOU'RE IN DETENTION!"

CHAPTER SIX

• • • • • •

Is the World Really a More Dangerous Place?

Little kids got beaten up by big kids even in the suburbs in the 1950s. It wasn't called mugging then, even if the kid took your wallet. The attitude I picked up from my parents was that you were a sissy if you were afraid of that sort of thing and that there were times when you had to fight back. But it's different living in the city. These are not just the neighbors' kids who are two years ahead, but kids you've never seen, maybe very disturbed and very dangerous. My 11-year-old son has to be aware of safe and not-safe areas and of who's around. He goes about where he has to go but he's very watchful. He has to be. I've never encouraged him to fight back. Even though he takes jujitsu, I've told him he should use it only if there is absolutely no other choice, no-where to run to.

—A FATHER

I don't worry so much about mugging. I worry more about robberies. We live in a safe suburban neighborhood, but we have a burglar alarm. All the houses do. (My parents never had an alarm. I don't think they even bothered to lock up at night.) My daughters are aware of it, too. If I forget to put the alarm on, one of them always reminds me. My greatest worry, though, is that a child-snatcher will lure my children or force them into a car. I worry partly because this is known

131

as a family neighborhood, the perfect place to come if you were that sick kind of person. And there was an incident with a little girl near here. So I tell my children not to talk to strangers. I tell them to scream if they need to. When I think that I used to be able to walk to school and my mother didn't worry. . . . I'd go out and play with my friends and she didn't even know where I was.

—A MOTHER

This last year my daughter has come home from school depressed about what's going to happen to the world that she's growing up in. She's not worried about nuclear war, but in social studies they talked a lot about pollution. I explained that every generation has its worries. In World War I, it was poison gasses. I told her that she can do her part by recycling and writing letters. (Just the other day she told me to stop using my hair spray!) But I think she still worries.

—A MOTHER

I remember watching the news once with my six-year-old and a particularly gruesome story came on. I said, ''Yuck. I shouldn't be letting you watch this,'' and she just laughed. I wasn't happy about it, but I wasn't prepared. When it's not a news show, but a regular TV show, I usually remind my kids that it's not real, that it's made up. I think the important thing is to make sure that they know that something might be scary, so they either can brace themselves or get back in touch with reality and not be bothered by it, or they can find some tactful reason for not watching, like, ''it's too boring.'' I don't worry that my kids will grow up to be murderers because of the violence on TV, but I do worry that it will make them nervous or unhappy.

—A FATHER

When Tom was in eighth grade we went to school for our parent-teacher conference and were looking through his journal. One entry said, "I sometimes wish I was never born." The teacher didn't think it meant anything, but we were very worried. He had seemed unhappy for a while, but we hadn't really focused on it. We found a therapist who helped him to work through these feelings, and we haven't seen any signs since. But we are always alert now.

—A FATHER

I was raised in a family that had just enough. My kids have so much more. We have wonderful vacations, we have a house at the beach. I think that kids are just accustomed to getting things they want. I see it even with myself. You have the money available to you and you spend it. It's not as if we're going to dress in sackcloth and ashes and give the rest of our money away. On the other hand, we try to convey to our children that we have a responsibility to people who have less than we do. We tell them that we send money to various organizations, and they know that I do some community work through their school. But I don't know how much of that sinks in. They also see what money can do, what you can have.

—A MOTHER

As a parent, I am always torn between the desire to shield my children and the belief that in order to grow up compassionate, they have to understand the whole spectrum of life. The more homogeneous the people you surround yourself with, the harder it is to trust other kinds of people. And if children are taught to be safe, they will be fearful. What I learned most from was Student CORE [Congress of Racial Equality] meetings in the 1960s, when I was working together with black kids. But kids also learn from their parents,

133

and my daughter knows that this is a family value. Last year, when my daughter had a free period to fill in school, she chose to be an aide in a special needs class. She told me, "My whole life I've been scared of retarded people, so I decided to work with them so that I won't be frightened anymore." I can't take credit for what she did but it delighted me.

—A MOTHER

Being a little kid in a big world was never easy, not even in the idealized 1950s. In fact, one child of the '50s, a mother now, recalls a girlhood of "preparing for air raids, not knowing if the Russians were going to drop the bomb on us." A father now in his 40s remembers vividly the polio epidemic that cast a shadow over one summer vacation and darkened much of his early childhood.

While polio has virtually disappeared in the Western world and a bombing strike by the Soviet Union seems less imminent than ever, other threats loom larger in children's minds. In 1987, for an annual survey by the Institute for Social Research of the University of Michigan, high school seniors across the nation were asked how often they worried about 11 specific problems facing the world. The problems that the greatest number of them worried about "sometimes" or "often" were crime and violence (81.9 percent), drug abuse (75 percent), hunger and poverty (62 percent), nuclear war (58 percent), economic problems (55 percent), pollution (45.2 percent), and race relations (44 percent).

Some experts believe that the present apprehensions of young people have been intensified by the high rate of divorce and their fear of it. "All children in today's world feel less protected," contends psychologist Dr. Judith Wallerstein, author of *Second Chances.* "Even those children raised in happy, intact families worry that their families may come undone.''

Children cannot be raised in glass bubbles, however, shielded from the world's problems. Even if they do not see violence, drugs, and poverty in their neighborhoods, they see them on their television screens. News broadcasts and other adult programs that many children regularly watch are filled with frightening images of the ravages of drugs, AIDS, war, urban violence, poverty, and homelessness, and the threats of nuclear holocaust and environmental destruction.

In order to walk the streets with confidence or to plan for the future with hope, children need the information, understanding, and practical skills that their parents are often best able to give them. (Some of these tools are described in this chapter and in the following two: What's New About Sex?'' and ''What's New About Drugs?'')

Parents cannot anticipate all the issues, crises, and problems their children will face, but they can encourage them to talk about any concerns or fears they have. Then together they can explore the choices children have and how to act on them. Children who are prepared for what might happen and who are assured of their parents' love and support, whatever does happen, will feel more control over their world.

Images of Violence

Parents can begin combatting their children's fears by focusing on the images and information they receive at home through television. By guiding children's television selections and watching programs together, parents can counter values they dislike and interpret information that is confusing or frightening.

When families watch television together, parents can look for opportunities after a show is over or during commercials to discuss what happened, to combat stereotypes, and to distinguish fantasy from reality for their children. In live-action shows, they can point out that real people could never recover so quickly and so completely from violent fights and accidents. They may also want to explain that stunts are staged with trained actors, trick shots, and specially rigged props and equipment. Nor should parents be complacent about Saturday morning cartoons—a staple for many young children. In these, animal and human characters often spring back to life unscathed from unimaginably violent treatment.

When violence is presented on television shows as a practical and acceptable solution to problems, parents can explain what the actual long-term emotional and legal consequences for people would be. They can discuss the moral implications of the characters' actions and work out with their children what the right or better solution might be in real life.

Some children are frightened by the violence they see on television. Parents should listen to their fears and allay them the best they can. They may explain that a dramatic story was made up by writers who wanted it to be as exciting and scary as possible so that people would watch. A news story on the other hand—such as a fire in which a whole family dies—also can be put into perspective. ''That is very sad,'' a father might say, ''but that kind of thing does not happen very often. We are lucky that our apartment building has never had a fire and that there are fire stairs we could use to get out if we had to.'' In general, parents should protect their children from seeing programs that they know will frighten them. Many children will accept with relief their parents' judgment that "This show is going to be too scary."

Although there is still controversy over the effects of television violence on children's behavior, this is often a prime concern of parents. In 1982, after reviewing 2,500 research studies, the National Institute of Mental Health concluded that watching violence on television increased aggressive behavior in children.

The impact of television violence, however, *is* affected by the family environment, according to Ellen Galinsky and Dr. Judy David in *The Preschool Years*. Its effect is lessened, they assert, when children are encouraged to play and read and when their parents watch television with them. In *Dr. Balter's Child Sense*, psychologist Lawrence Balter, Ph.D., raises another issue. "As far as I'm concerned," he writes, "violent content is not good for a young child—not only because it may teach him violence—but because it desensitizes him to the inhumanity of the violence."

Because much of what appears on television is not appropriate for children, many parents monitor the shows that their children watch and limit viewing to certain special programs. As Martin D. Franks, a vice president of CBS, stated (*New York Times*, August 23, 1989), "The bottom line is [that] consumers vote on our programming several times every night when they hit their remote control button. If the public thinks there is too much sex on television or too much violence on television, the best way to get it off is not to watch it." Some concerned parents have joined Action for Children's Television (20 University Road, Cambridge, MA 02138), a national organization that works to improve the quality of television programming.

By limiting the amount of time their children spend watching television, parents can make sure that their lives are not consumed by this activity as well as convey to them their own priorities. To be effective, though, parents must offer an attractive alternative—tossing a ball in the back-yard, for instance, or reading a story together—so that turn-ing off the television is not perceived as a punishment. They should reinforce this message through their own viewing habits and use of leisure time.

Personal Safety

Crime *has* grown worse since today's parents were chil-dren, in rural and suburban areas as well as in large cities. In *How to Raise a Street-Smart Child,* author Grace Hechinger states that, according to the Uniform Crime Reports of the FBI, the chance of being the victim of a major violent crime (murder, rape, robbery, aggravated assault) or of a serious crime against property nearly tripled between 1960 and 1976. Then from 1976 to 1988, property crime rose only about 4 percent, but the estimated rate of violent crimes, based on those reported, rose by about 36 percent. In ad-dition, according to psychologist Nicholas Ziff, Ph.D., and demographer Carolyn C. Rogers in their essay, "Recent Trends in the Well-Being of Children in the United States and Their Implications for Public Policy" (in *The Changing American Family and Public Policy,* edited by Andrew J. Cher-lin), during the 1980s victimization rates for children aged 12 to 19 were about twice as high as those for adults.

Violence is most prevalent, however, in this nation's in-ner cities. In "Growing Up Scared" (*Atlantic,* June 1990), writer Karl Zinsmeister reported that a recent study of inner-city teenagers in Baltimore found that 24 percent had witnessed a murder, 72 percent knew someone who had been shot, and most had seen or had been victims of some kind of violence.

Hechinger encourages parents, when discussing the problem of crime with their children, to "always emphasize what children should do to protect themselves, never the bad things that might happen to them." Otherwise they may be so paralyzed by fear that they never learn how to act safely.

Children can learn the rules of personal safety in the same ways that they learn the rules of health or of traffic or fire safety. Some parents use as teaching tools experiences from their own childhoods, incidents that happened in the neighborhood, or events that were reported on television. Experts also recommend playing the "What if . . . ?" game ("What would you do if you thought someone was following you down the street?" "What would you do if a bigger kid told you to give him your money?" "What would you do if you were home alone and the doorbell rang?"). Parents should listen to the child's reaction and discuss it before presenting other possible solutions. Then they can decide together on the best plan. But that should not be the end of it. Safety talks, like school fire drills, need to be repeated over and over so that children will respond automatically.

Almost more important than any specific safety rules, however, is how these rules are conveyed. An underlying message of "They're out to get you!" or "Run for your life!" is likely to create terror and may prevent children from becoming independent. A better message for children to hear is that they can master the dangers in their world by using their common sense and learning certain safety rules. These might include staying alert, walking on well-lighted blocks, coming home before dark, traveling with a friend, or seeking help from someone in a uniform—whatever good judgement dictates for the age and maturity of the child and for the area in which the family lives. With this knowledge, children will be more confident about moving around in the outside world.

Children also should be encouraged to trust their in-stincts. "Did you ever have a funny feeling about a person or a place but didn't know what was the matter?" a parent might ask. "That uncomfortable feeling is your body's way of telling you that something is wrong. If you ever get a funny feeling about something or someone, do not ignore it, even if that means being rude." Some children compro-mise their safety by trying to be polite. They should know that if ever they think they might be in danger, they are allowed to lie, to disobey adults, to hit, bite, and scream in order to get away.

The issue of strangers is another aspect of safety training. Many children picture a stranger as a ghoul, rather than a nice-looking, friendly man or woman. Parents should ex-plain to children that a stranger is anyone they do not know or whom they know only by name or occupation. "Most adults like children and are nice to them," they might add. "But a few are not nice, and you can't tell by how they look. That's why we have rules about strangers." Some parents use an animal analogy. "You don't pet every dog you see on the street because even some cute dogs bite. If you want to pet a dog, you ask Mom or Dad first." In *The Safe Child Book,* author Sherryll Kerns Kraizer recommends teaching children four rules: Stay more than an arm's reach away from strangers; don't talk to strangers; don't take anything from strangers; and don't go anywhere with strangers.

Adults should always praise children for following safety rules, even when the rules cause inconvenience or embar-rassment. One 10-year-old boy refused to open the door on a cold winter day to a friend of his uncle's because he wasn't told to expect her. When the uncle arrived and his freezing friend was finally let in, her first words to the boy were, "What a terrific kid! You did just the right thing."

Likewise, a child who is the victim of a crime should

never be made to feel responsible or ashamed about what happened. If a mugger steals a bike or a watch, for instance, parents need to replace it immediately, if possible. They should report the crime to the police or the school and encourage the child to be angry at the criminal, not at himself. Parents also may want to tell their children that crimes, like sickness, sometimes happen to people for no reason at all, not because they deserve it.

Sexual Abuse and Abduction

Although many parents worry that their child may be abducted by a stranger, the danger is actually very small. According to journalist John Crewdson in *By Silence Betrayed*, more than 90 percent of children reported to the police as missing are runaways who are found or return home within a few days. Of those who are still missing after several weeks, most who are not runaways were taken by a parent in a custody dispute.

Sexual abuse, however, is much more prevalent. In a random national survey of more than 2,500 Americans conducted by the *Los Angeles Times* in July 1985, 22 percent reported that they were victims of sexual abuse when they were children. One-third of them had told no one at the time it happened.

Children need more than safety rules to protect them from sexual abuse. First, they need information about their bodies—accurate names for their genitals and explanations about sexuality that they can understand. Knowing that these subjects can be discussed with their parents will help to remove any aura of shame or secrecy connected with children's bodies or their sexual thoughts and feelings. Parents also need to explain to children the difference between a secret, which is meant never to be told, and a surprise, which is usually shared. Children should know that it is wrong for adults to ask them to keep secrets of a sexual nature, and that they are right to betray such a trust, even if they break a promise.

Through their actions as well as their words, parents need to give the message to even very young children that "Your body belongs to you. If you don't want to be touched, you have the right to say so and I will support you." This rule must apply as much to sweet old Granny who is only ask-. ing for a good-bye kiss as to the stranger at the store. "I respect this in my office," writes pediatrician and child development expert Dr. T. Berry Brazelton in *Working and Caring*, "always asking [my young patients] for their permission to examine them. I never ask them to take their underpants completely off, 'because that part of your body is special, and you might like to keep it covered.' "

Since it is estimated that three-quarters of sexual abusers are known to their victims, children also need to be told that grown-ups can make mistakes. "A baby-sitter or a teacher or a police officer might ask you to do something you know you shouldn't," the parent might say, and then ask some "What ifs." ("What if your teacher asked you to climb onto the roof of the school and jump off?" "What if Uncle Marty was tickling you and you didn't like it?") Children can be taught to respect those in authority and still learn when to question an adult's words or actions.

Some experts recommend teaching children that there are different kinds of touches: good touches (loving and comforting), bad touches (such as hits and punches, which hurt), and confusing touches (which make you feel funny). Since these distinctions may be unclear, however, others believe it is better to empower children to rebuff any contact they do not want.

The best way for parents to ensure their children's safety

is to listen to them and watch them carefully. Quietly pursue complaints about a baby-sitter, a relative, the unexplained appearance of a new toy, the mention of a secret, or possible signs of sexual abuse, including a change in personality or behavior, physical symptoms, or a heightened interest in anything sexual. Most important, parents should believe children when they say they have been abused, no matter who the abuser is; reassure them of their love and protection; and insist that what happened was not their fault. Experts encourage parents to get help for the child from a mental health professional and to report the molester to the police in order to protect others.

Prejudice

In our society today, serious intergroup tensions still exist and even seem to be worsening in some urban areas. Many television shows still reinforce old stereotypes of women, racial and ethnic groups, religious groups, the elderly, and the handicapped. News programs often focus unfavorably and unfairly on a whole group because of a single incident, or in order to enhance exciting details. In *Teaching and Learning in a Diverse World*, Patricia Ramsey, Ed.D., assistant professor of psychology and education at Mt. Holyoke College, states, "When people of color and poor people are shown . . . , it is usually related to hunger, poverty, a crime, or a disaster." Some parents worry that in such a world their children will grow up prejudiced and uncaring, fearful and hateful of people who are different from them, or will become victims of prejudice themselves.

Parents should be reminded that they have a strong influence on their children's attitudes, positive and negative. "Probably one of the most difficult responsibilities parents have," author-educator Dolores Curran writes in *Traits of a Healthy Family*, "is to teach their children to respect people with whom the parents disagree or whom they basically fear. . . . Otherwise good and loving parents frequently bump into their own bigotry in this area. . . . Then the respect they've taught is really selective, limited respect."

Experts recommend that teaching tolerance can never start too soon. By the age of three, children are aware of skin color; by five or six they recognize other differences in appearance and behavior. According to Dr. Ramsey, the period between ages three and eight is when children's early perceptions of differences form into more permanent attitudes.

Parents' accepting attitudes can help children learn to be open and tolerant. Parents can explain unfamiliar behavior or physical handicaps and show children that the appropriate response to differences should be interest rather than revulsion. A young child, for example, might report to his mother about a classmate from Japan: "Yohei's gross. He eats seaweed—yuck!" The mother could counter this reaction by explaining that seaweed is not very different from spinach and that in a country like Japan, which is surrounded by the ocean, it is a natural source of nutrition. "It might be fun to try some," she might add. "You could ask him to tell us where we can buy it."

Parents can introduce even young children to aspects of different cultures. They can try special ethnic foods and observe how other people celebrate holidays in this country and abroad. Families can read books together about people from different ethnic, racial, and religious backgrounds and talk about the experiences and struggles they may have had. Children can learn to take pride in their *own* culture and tradition. The underlying message, however, should be that no group of people is better than another. Although eight- or nine-year-old children cannot understand that their way of doing things is only one among many choices, according to Dr. Ramsey, they usually are open to new experiences. ''Later, when they can understand cultural relativity,'' she writes, ''they will have more content and experience to support these insights.''

Through these experiences and through opportunities to play with different kinds of children and to see their parents socialize with the other parents, children can learn that all people have much in common. Psychologists have found that children and adults are more inclined to like and to help people whom they perceive to be similar to themselves than those whom they see as being different. In *Bringing up a Moral Child*, psychologists Dr. Michael Schulman and Eva Mekler write, ''There is probably no more important lesson you can teach your child than that 'us' is all of humanity, all races, all religions, all nationalities.''

Tolerance of others' differences, according to Schulman and Mekler, is a direct result of empathy, the ability to understand another person's point of view, separate from one's own. Although psychologists do not agree on the age at which children fully develop empathy, even very young children respond to the emotions of others, offering a doll to a child in tears or crying themselves when another child is upset. Children who can see members of other groups as people like themselves, with feelings and problems, are less likely to avoid, fear, or ridicule them.

Parents can foster empathy by drawing attention to the feelings of others whenever possible. (''It hurts when you bounce on me so hard,'' or ''Look at that sad little boy. Why do you think he is crying?'') Older children could be encouraged to think about how prejudice and discrimination affect others they may have never met by discussing events in the news.

Parents can also emphasize to their children how highly they value tolerance and caring. They can point out as models kind people they know or people who have received attention in the community or in the media for their good deeds. Parents also can praise their children whenever they act kindly and highlight their own acts of empathy by explaining what they are doing and why ("Aunt Millie is feeling lonely these days without Uncle Hank, so I invited her to come on the trip with us. Can you think of some way to make her feel especially welcome?").

Unfortunately, Grace Hechinger warns, distrust of people from racial and ethnic groups whose members are disproportionately poor tends to exist when crime rates are high. She encourages parents to try to explain to children that when people are poor, they are more likely to commit street crimes, and when one whole group of people is poorer than other groups, more of them are likely to break the law. She adds that "children at an early age can be made to understand that while crime cannot be condoned, it is everybody's duty to help eliminate discrimination and other conditions that keep some groups in poverty." Parents should point out that most people from whatever group their children may fear are not criminals and give examples of people in that group who are liked and admired. They can point out that good people in a group are less likely to get publicity than the evildoers because their stories are less sensational. Children who themselves have experienced discrimination also should be encouraged not to generalize unfairly or to dismiss a whole group because of an ugly experience with one individual.

Haves and Have Nots

In the 1970s and 1980s especially, Americans became very intent on attaining personal gratification, achieving success, and acquiring possessions. This attitude conflicts with compassion for those who are less fortunate and discourages any selfless commitment to helping others. It also is reflected in the goals and values of many young people. According to Dr. Zill and Rogers in their essay in *The Changing American Family and Public Policy*, surveys indicate that young people today tend to be "more focused on material success, less concerned about social justice, and less reflective about the meaning and purpose of life."

To begin to combat the trend toward materialism, psychologist Charles E. Schaefer, Ph.D., advises parents in *How to Talk to Children About Really Important Things* not to connect money with love or use it for a reward. They should resist trying to buy their children's affection with grand gifts. This never works and only invests material goods with an undue importance. They also should not pay their children for good grades, a practice that belittles the real rewards of learning.

Since television commercials are powerful agents of materialism, parents may want to explain to their children how ads can create the desire for unnecessary products. Once alerted, many children enjoy ferreting out the devious methods of advertisers. Parents may also want to discuss wiser choices for spending money.

Sometimes young people seem uninterested in helping others simply because they do not know how. Children learn most from their parents, by observing how they spend their time and money and how giving they are in their relationships. A child whose mother works in a soup kitchen once a week is more likely to volunteer to help others. A child who sees his father do favors ungrudgingly for his friends is more likely to be generous himself. Parents can also talk to their children about what they are doing and why, including the pleasure it gives them to help others.

Parents who contribute money to charitable organizations also can use this as an opportunity to teach their children how money can be spent unselfishly. They can explain their reasons for supporting certain causes and can correct the misconception some children have that people who are suffering did something to deserve their misfortune or are inferior in some way.

Some parents include a small charity fund in their children's allowance and encourage them to donate money regularly. They may describe a number of charities and let the children choose. Young children are often attracted to groups that help animals or children. Parents who expect their children to give to charities are teaching them that some people have less than others, often through no fault of their own, but that a bond of caring and responsibility exists among all people.

Many preteens and teenagers are old enough to benefit from volunteer work at community organizations (hospitals, homeless shelters, churches, humane societies, or city recreation departments), though they may need their parents' help to find the right job. By helping senior citizens or disabled children, or working with groups to clean up parks or beaches, children learn that their skills and energies can make a difference in people's lives. At the same time, they may lose some of their distrust or fear of people who are different from or less fortunate than they.

The Future of the Planet

For the next generation of children, fears of acid rain and chemical waste may replace the fears of nuclear attack that their parents may have had growing up. On the other hand, what adults today view with relief as a vast reduction in the nuclear threat is only a reduction by comparison. To children, the huge world nuclear arsenal could still seem terrifying.

In *The Strangelove Legacy*, which explores children's concerns about survival in a nuclear age, writer Phyllis La Farge reports that young adolescents between the ages of 12 and 14 are the most vulnerable to fears of nuclear war. They know more facts than younger children, but cannot yet think abstractly, as older teens do. As a result, they cannot distance themselves from the issue. "The young adolescent's still limited sense of social institutions increases his sense of helplessness and therefore his anxiety and pessimism about nuclear war," she writes. "His still quite concrete way of thinking does not allow him a very developed understanding of the way people can work together to prevent war." She also suggests that although the nuclear issue is unique, her findings may apply to environmental and other "big world" problems as well.

She encourages parents to give their children tools to face these complex issues. Children can learn at home what the facts are and how to make judgments about policies and leaders. Parents can look for opportunities, such as at dinnertime or while watching a relevant television program, to discuss public issues and to listen to and answer their children's questions. Even if the answer is "I don't know," parents can help their children find out. They also can describe to their children what they do, if anything, about these issues, and outline actions the children themselves can take, be it writing a letter, raising money, joining an activist organization, or gathering more information.

Some environmental issues can be tackled at home, and there are concrete actions children can take. In *50 Simple Things Kids Can Do to Save the Earth*, John Javna writes, "In our experience, kids are not only willing but very eager to do their part. But they need information, encouragement, and—this is the important one—the sense that they have the power to make a difference." He goes on to describe what children can do. They can turn off lights when they are not using them, for example, and wash dishes in a basin instead of under running water. They can "adopt" an endangered animal and help separate garbage for recycling.

Parents also can help their children by putting their fears into context. To children worried about carcinogens in their food and environment, for instance, they can point out that although there are small amounts of these cancer-causing agents in some substances, many of the most potent ones have been identified and are being regulated.

The most harmful response to children's fears about the future—as to their questions about any emotionally sensitive subject—is no answer at all. Silence suggests a dark, dangerous secret and encourages children to keep their worries to themselves. And what children don't know, most experts warn, *can* hurt them.

Suicide

After accidents, suicide is the second leading cause of death among adolescents. According to "The Index of Social Health for Children and Youth," prepared by the Fordham Institute for Innovations in Social Policy, the suicide rate doubled between 1970 and 1987. Some experts have been quick to match this rise in suicide with the higher rates of divorce and of working mothers. But others point out that suicide rates for adults in their 20s and 30s have risen also, so that there is probably a broader cause.

Doctors, psychologists, and social scientists have all offered explanations of why teenagers—or adults—commit suicide, few of which would probably satisfy the families of the victims. Some blame inherited tendencies or the absence of certain chemicals in the brain; others blame drug and alcohol abuse. Some point to the pressure on young people today to grow up quickly and achieve success or on the bleak outlook they may have on the future in a world with overwhelming problems. Still others blame the media for sensationalizing and romanticizing accounts of teenage suicides.

Most experts agree, however, that depression is often at the root of suicidal feelings. Depression causes a sadness much deeper and longer lasting than is warranted by any external circumstances. If a child's depressed feelings last more than two weeks, are very intense, or prompt talk about suicide, parents should seek professional help immediately, for depression can be treated effectively with psychotherapy, medication, and other techniques.

Families that encourage openness and communication and have always offered ways to confront and solve problems together may believe that their children will never need to harbor thoughts of suicide. For reasons no one understands, this is not always so. All parents, therefore, should be aware of the following events and subtle clues that may signal a child in trouble:

- A change in behavior or personality
- A change in eating and sleeping habits
- A change in school performance
- Increased use of drugs and alcohol
- Risk taking
- The giving away of personal treasures
- A great personal loss
- The death or attempted suicide of a friend or loved one
- A preoccupation with death and dying
- Talking about suicide or a wish to die

- Expressing feelings of great sadness and hopelessness (these may disappear suddenly if the child decides to commit suicide)

Individually, the items on this list may seem to be normal adolescent experiences and behaviors. The best indications that they may be much more serious are their intensity, duration, or appearance in a cluster. In these instances, parents should get help quickly.

A Better World

Many children can accept the world as it is today more easily than can their parents because they have no memory of a world that seemed safer and less complex. Some children, however, are fearful and worry about a variety of world problems. The best help parents can give them is to listen to and treat their fears seriously. Then they can assure their children that solutions can be found, just as they have in the past, especially if people work together. Parents can also give their children hope and a sense of power by helping them to find ways to participate actively in solving the problems that worry them and in creating a better world.

CHAPTER SEVEN

• • • • • •

What's New About Sex?

What I learned about sex I learned from friends. It was something the guys would talk about in school. The only time I remember the topic coming up at home was once when I was a senior in high school. I was going out of the house to pick up my girlfriend and my mother said, ''I assume you know everything you need to know.'' I said, ''Yeah, I guess so,'' and that was the end of it. But I really didn't know very much. Now things are so different. Kids see so much— the sexual stimulation is phenomenal—and, with birth control, the availability of sex has increased tremendously.

When our two boys were little, they would ask questions about the differences between girls and boys, and about pregnant women they saw on the street. We would explain, but we never got into any explicit discussion at that age. But when my oldest son was about nine, my wife said, ''Don't you think it's time?'' My reaction was, ''You've got to be kidding!'' But we sat him down and we started off the conversation with how, as you get older, your body changes. We discussed sexual intercourse and birth. He knew it all already! Out of curiosity I kept going. I had to get to wet dreams before I was able to say anything that surprised him.

Sex never has been a subject of detailed conversations between us, though. When Michael was a senior in high school and found a girlfriend, I told him about birth control. I didn't talk about it before because he wasn't really dating heavily and we didn't think there was any need for it. He listened, but I had the sense that most of it he had already heard elsewhere. I emphasized that sex is a very serious matter because a girl can get pregnant and that is an amazingly large responsibility. This may have been a way on my part to put pressure on him—to tell him to hold off for a while. We also told him that we really didn't want him in his bedroom with his girlfriend. It was our way of saying that we didn't think he was ready to have sex.

I didn't get into the moral issues of how you treat somebody, because I have always had confidence in both of my kids being decent people. The only time I did that was when my younger son broke up with his girlfriend. I was shocked because of the way he did it—so abruptly—and I told him that some day it was going to happen to him and he would understand the pain he had caused. Nonetheless, I'm sure something very dramatic must have happened even then.

Now both of my sons are in college. I don't know whether they are still virgins or not. I'd almost say that once a kid is that age, it's none of a parent's business. But I don't know how I'd feel if I had a daughter. I'm sure I have a double standard.

—A FATHER

My parents never told me anything. All my mother ever told me were things like "Save it for the one you love," and "It's the most precious gift you can give a man"—that's a quote from my mother. Anything I learned about sex I learned at summer camp when I was nine or 10. The girls would talk at night in the bunk, and I would just lie in bed amazed at what intercourse was.

I got a lot of misinformation from my friends. When I was 16 or 17, I remember worrying that I could get pregnant because a guy ejaculated when we were making out or that I could get pregnant because I sat on a guy's lap in my bathing suit.

154

When my kids were about five and six, my husband told them the whole story about sex, even though I am of the school that you give answers to the questions children ask only as fully as they ask them. I believe my kids have learned a lot in school about the physical dynamics: where everything is and how it works, about danger, and about protection. But the other issue I want my kids to understand is feelings. Magazines that kids read tell them how to "do it." Kids also see a lot that we didn't—on TV, in the movies, even in ads. But the context is not one that conveys the feeling you would want, so you still have to talk to them yourself. They need to be aware that they can hurt other people. They need to think about the meaning of sex.

At puberty my daughter didn't want to talk about herself. She was more interested in what I did as a teenager and what my attitude about sex was. I talked to her mostly about feelings. I told her that I made out with a boy heavily for the first time when I was in the seventh grade. I said I felt that experience was more than I could handle emotionally, and that it was several years before I found someone I could care about very, very much.

The issue for her is not so much about sex and what happens. It is how you find someone in this world of divorce and separation whom you can stay with, and whether she will ever find this person. That concerns and frightens her. She's in the ninth grade now and in a fickle phase. I tell her that I was fickle once, as she is now, and that you move through stages of relationships. You don't get married when you're 12 or 14. You're not experienced enough. From each relationship you learn something. You have a lot of experiences and that's the normal way of doing it. Sometimes I don't say anything. I just listen. She only wants to know ultimately that she's normal, that these feelings have been felt before, and that she's a good person.

Judging from her group of friends, I'd say that kids are

becoming more conservative. They are becoming more careful about feelings as well as about the medical issues.

—A MOTHER

The birds and the bees are still doing what birds and bees have always done. In that sense, there is nothing at all new to say about sex. But there have been changes, some good, some bad, over the past generation. If parents try to understand these changes and the effects they have on children growing up today, they will be better able to help their children develop into healthy, sexual adults. They also will be better able to instill values about other important aspects of human relationships. It is no less important today than in the past to treat others with kindness, honesty, and respect, to have respect for oneself, and to take responsibility for one's actions. Children who learn these values from their parents will apply them to their sexual behavior as well as to other parts of their lives.

The Sexual Revolution

When *Seventeen* magazine was first published in 1944, a certification preceded certain stories: "This has been read by your pastor and a teacher, and approved for your reading." In 1988, when the teen magazine *Sassy* made its debut, the lineup of articles included such titles as "The Truth About Boys' Bodies," "How to Kiss," and "Laural and Lesli and Alex and Brian: They're dating. They go to movies and concerts. They fight over stupid things. They make up. They're sad sometimes. They're happy. AND THEY'RE GAY."

Many people trace the dramatic shift in sexual openness to the 1960s, when young people rebelled against all kinds of authority, including authority over sexual behavior. "If it feels good, do it!" was the rallying cry of at least a vocal minority. But the roots of the sexual revolution go deeper. In the late 1940s and early 1950s, Alfred Kinsey, Sc.D., brought sex out of the closet and into the public forum with his surveys of adult sexual behavior. He also pricked a balloon of hypocrisy when he revealed that many people were not practicing what they preached. A great many married couples, for instance, even in long-term marriages, were having more varied sex and finding it mutually satisfying. Many more people than was generally believed engaged in premarital or extramarital sexual relationships. This first frank discussion of sexual behavior opened the way for the more clinical observations and scientific measurements of researchers William Masters, M.D., and Virginia Johnson in the 1960s.

Support for a more relaxed attitude toward sex came from other directions as well. Psychoanalysts warned that too much sexual restraint could lead to neurosis. Anthropologists catalogued the wide range of sexual behavior considered appropriate by people in different cultures. Women began to attack the double standard that allowed good boys to sow their wild oats but required good girls to say no. Finally, the development of antibiotics limited the risk involved in acquiring sexually transmitted diseases, and access to reliable birth control removed the most powerful practical restraint, the fear of pregnancy. Meanwhile, the declining influence of religion eliminated some of the moral restraints to premarital sex.

Young people today become interested in sex earlier than in the past partly because they grow up faster. Because of better nutrition and health care in industrialized countries, the average age when boys and girls become sexually mature has declined continually since the beginning of the century. In the early 1900s in America, the average age of menarche (a girl's first period) was 14. Now it is just over 12. Boys today, on the average, are sexually mature at 13. Since some of the physical and emotional changes may begin as much as two years before sexual maturity, some children today are experiencing signs of puberty before the age of 10.

In modern society, however, physical maturity is not the ticket to adulthood. Children must be self-sufficient before they marry and begin to raise a family. Paradoxically, while children's bodies have matured earlier, the duration of their dependence on parents has grown longer. For many of today's adolescents, the increasing delay in emotional maturity and the added difficulty of obtaining financial security result in marriage at a later age than in the past. Thus, young people today are sexually active at an earlier age and for a longer time before marriage than any previous generation. Changing attitudes also encourage this situation. A sizable segment of the population does not consider premarital sex immoral; a woman who is not a virgin no longer is tainted; teenagers are much more open about sex than they were 30 years ago. Few parents today would be shocked to hear that their neighbor took her teenage daughter to a clinic for birth control counseling.

Recently, however, signs have appeared to indicate that the sexual revolution has crested. Even Hugh Hefner, creator of *Playboy* magazine, has married and settled down, and *Oh, Calcutta!*, the irreverent nude Broadway show, finally closed after 6,000 performances. The swinging single who hops from one sexual adventure to another is no longer quite the glamorous hero of movies and television shows. The camera seems to be shifting a more favorable focus toward those who seek commitment. Some observers point to the threat of AIDS (Acquired Immune Deficiency Syndrome) as the cause. But in *AIDS and Its Metaphors,* social critic Susan Sontag argues that there is ''a broad tendency in our culture, an end-of-the-era feeling, that AIDS is reinforcing; an exhaustion, for many, of purely secular ideals. . . . [T]he behavior AIDS is stimulating is part of a larger grateful return to what is perceived as 'conventions,' the reduction in the imperative of promiscuity in the middle class, a growth of the ideal of monogamy, of a prudent sexual life. . . .''

Whatever it signals about the future, however, right now both AIDS and a high teenage pregnancy rate require openness about sexuality between parents and children. Because teenagers today have more freedom, they also have more pressures and more decisions to make. They need their parents' guidance.

Media Sex

Sex is a subject virtually impossible to ignore. Headlines in newspapers and on nightly news programs overflow with words children rarely heard when most of today's parents were growing up: abortion, rape, child abuse, pornography, homosexuality, AIDS. Sex is the subject of popular songs, movies, television shows, and advertisements. Children pass newsstands filled with pornographic magazines in which women and men are displayed as objects, and they watch rock videos, which often associate sex with violence.

What do children learn from this inundation? From television shows they learn that love relationships develop instantly, that no one worries about birth control and pregnancy, and that people who barely know each other have sexual intercourse. They also learn from advertising that the goal of many men and almost all women is to look, act, and smell sexy.

Since it is impossible to ship children off to a Himalayan monastery until they are 20, the best way for parents to protect them is to meet the media enemy head-on. They can watch television with their children and discuss together what they see. An evening of prime-time television could easily elicit provocative questions, such as: ''Do you think what that man did was right?'', ''How would you feel if someone treated you that way?'', ''What do you think would really happen if that man and woman didn't use birth control?'', and ''Do you know what rape means?'' For years concerned parents have been explaining to their children the sly tricks advertisers use to make their products appear more attractive than they really are. Children will learn their parents' attitudes toward sex if parents also take the time to criticize and comment thoughtfully on what children see on television and in movies. Through discussion, parents can teach their children to interpret the hidden messages about relationships that much of the media promotes.

R-rated movies and ads for perfume and jeans are not the only sources of topics for fruitful discussion. Commercials for breakfast cereals or detergents showing family scenes are also rife with sexual suggestions. After all, sexuality is much more than the act of intercourse. It includes gender, body image, family roles—the entire experience of being male or female. ''How come the detergent commercials show mainly boys roughhousing, causing trouble, and getting dirty?'' parents might ask. ''What are they saying about what boys and girls are like and what they do?''

Sex Education: Whose Job?

Although most parents believe children should learn about sexuality at home, many are relieved that the subject is being taught in school by trained teachers. Partly in response to public concern about AIDS, there has been a significant increase in the amount of sex education offered by schools in the last five years. By 1989 sex education was required or encouraged in more than 40 states. What is taught, however, is often too little and comes too late. These classes usually are not offered until the ninth or tenth grade, and only as a small unit (about 11 hours) of a yearlong health or biology course. They also usually focus narrowly on the physiological aspects of sex.

Some parents are still reluctant to allow schools to discuss birth control, abortion, safe sex, and homosexuality, and some teachers themselves are not comfortable with these topics. Opponents of sex education stir fears that children will view the imparting of information as an adult endorsement of sexual activity and become promiscuous. Yet according to the Planned Parenthood Federation of America manual, *How to Talk With Your Child About Sexuality*, a number of studies have proved the reverse: Adolescent girls who are given frank and thorough information about human sexuality become pregnant by accident much less often than those who are not informed. They also are likely to begin sexual relations at a later age.

Many experts recommend that sex education begin in kindergarten, or at least by the age of seven. In Sweden, a country recognized as a leader in the field of sex education, programs begin in preschool and extend through secondary school. Swedish parents also are encouraged to provide information. The effectiveness of this approach is probably reflected by the teenage pregnancy rate in Sweden, which is less than half that of the United States. A study by Sol Gordon, Ph.D., former professor of child and family studies at Syracuse University, also found that more than 80 percent of Scandinavian teenagers use birth control when they first have intercourse. In the United States, by comparison, fewer than 20 percent of sexually active teenagers use contraception the first time they have sex and only 30 percent use reliable contraception after that.

American parents also are not doing their job. In *Raising a Child Conservatively in a Sexually Permissive World*, coauthors Dr. Sol Gordon and Judith Gordon note that in a survey of 450 Syracuse University undergraduates, only about 10 percent of the respondents answered that their parents had discussed sex honestly with them. Some parents claim that they don't know how to talk about sex with their children; after all, their own parents didn't provide them with models of how to do this well, or in some cases, at all.

Yet the most salient learning about sexuality can take place naturally, not as a formal lecture. Parents who cuddle their infants are telling them without words that their bodies are wonderful and are encouraging them to be sensual in a healthy way. Parents who show affection toward each other openly and lovingly are teaching their children to associate sexuality with comfort and happiness.

But the key to sex education at home is communication—listening as well as talking. Parents should convey the message that sexuality is a normal part of life, which they are happy to discuss with their children. So long as the lines of communication are open, parents can try to transmit accurate information and try to influence their children's behavior. This process starts early, by answering questions calmly and honestly and anticipating unasked questions. With shyer children or at shyer ages, parents will have to look for "teachable moments." After visiting a friend's new baby, one mother asked her seven-year-old if he knew how babies were born. "He said, 'No, and I don't care!' so vehemently that I knew he cared a lot," she said. "And I realized that it was time to talk about it."

Parents also need to make sure that their children understand and know what to expect *before* physical changes occur in their bodies. With older children, humor can help overcome embarrassment. One father who had overheard his 12-year-old son talking to his friends about condoms joked to the boy that a deflated balloon they saw looked like a huge condom. He wanted to let his son know that this was a subject he could ask about if he wanted more information.

At every age, the questions change and the answers have to be tailored to the child's understanding. The usual rule of thumb is that if children are curious enough to ask the questions, they are old enough to hear the answers. If a four-year-old asks what AIDS is, for instance, a parent might say that it is a very serious disease and reassure him that there is very little chance either he or his parents will get it. By about the age of nine, children usually are ready to hear the specific facts of transmission and prevention.

Traditionally mothers have talked to their children about sex, or a mother would talk to a daughter and a father to a son. Today experts recommend that both parents be involved. Delegating the job to Mom reinforces the notion that sexual matters are a woman's concern and that males are not responsible. And if mothers and fathers talk only to the same-sex child, they may convey the idea that men and women cannot or should not discuss sex together. This also cuts off an important source of information and a valuable point of view. One couple bought their 11-year-old son a book about sexuality written for preteens and teenagers and alternated reading chapters aloud to him at bedtime. "I thought he might have questions about girls that I could answer better than his father," the mother said, "and he did." On the other hand, another boy might be uncomfortable talking about these matters with his mother, and that feeling, too, should be respected.

As with any aspect of child rearing, parents should discuss and agree beforehand on what they will say and how and their expectations for their children's sexual behavior. Reflecting on their own experiences and feelings about sexuality can be enlightening and provide insights on how to talk to their children.

Parents who are uncomfortable discussing sexual topics should also feel free to admit their feelings to their children ("It's not so easy for me to talk to you about this, but it's important"). While it can be helpful for parents to share some of their own experiences as an adolescent or adult, if asked, it is also fine to say, "These are very personal questions and I don't feel comfortable discussing my sex life with you." In fact, although they may ask, most teenagers would be upset to hear the details of their parents' sex lives.

Parents also have to be realistic about the limits of their influence over children as they get older. For adolescents, the sexual standards of their peers wield great power over their behavior. What parents *can* influence, however, are the *moral* aspects of their children's relationships. Values about how to treat other people are learned from a child's earliest social experiences onward, starting with the playpen and the sandbox.

Recently experts have been stressing the connection between self-esteem and sexual behavior. Teenagers with high self-esteem respect themselves and expect to be treated with respect. Those with low self-esteem may give in to sexual pressures from a partner or their peer group in the hope of winning acceptance. The building of self-esteem begins early in a child's life. The best way to foster it is simply for parents to show their children how much they love and value them in as many ways and as often as possible. Allowing children to be independent and to make decisions on their own, helping them to develop their talents and special abilities, and praising them sincerely and often all encourage their sense of competence.

The combination of a full understanding of sexuality and a secure sense of self-esteem is also the best protection parents can provide their children from sexual abuse by an adult or an older child. In addition, parents should arm them from an early age with the right to say, "My body belongs to me." They should know that no one—a stranger, a neighbor, a relative, a friend—has the right to touch or fondle them against their will. A child can be told, "If you don't like the way someone touches you, say so. And if it happens anyway, tell someone else—even if you promised not to."

The ABCs of Sexuality

Children are born sexual. Babies begin to learn about physical and emotional love from their parents at birth, and they learn early that touching certain parts of their bodies is especially pleasurable. When they are two or three they usually become interested in exploring the difference between boys and girls. This curiosity is natural and healthy, and just one way that young children use their senses to learn about the world and themselves. They can be given opportunities to see other boys and girls naked and parents might point out the anatomical differences. There are also anatomically correct dolls that parents can purchase for children.

Parents can begin the process of informing and communicating with their children at a young age by using the proper names for body parts rather than using confusing babyish euphemisms they might have learned as children. This can be done casually while dressing, undressing, or bathing a child, with the goal that some day he will be able to ask a parent why his penis hurts (or why it is not as big as his older brother's) just as comfortably as he might say that he has an earache.

For parents who wish to, there is nothing wrong with occasionally using made-up terms for male and female genitals, as they might for other body parts, as long as their children also know the correct terms. Parents should be warned, however, that around the age of two, children enjoy naming body parts and will do so at every opportunity, especially, it seems, in public! This may be embarrassing for the adult in charge, but it should be less so if the child uses straightforward language like *penis* and *buttocks* rather than words like *winkie* and *tush*. In any case, by about the age of three or four, most children can understand the concepts of private and public and what is appropriate for each.

If children ask why boys have penises and girls don't, parents can explain that what boys have is right for them and what girls have is right for them and just as good. With any questions of this nature, whatever the age of the children, parents should ask, "What do you think?" before they give an answer in order to gauge what kind of information children want and what misinformation they may already have.

Playing doctor is one way young children explore sexual differences. Usually these games do no harm, but instead help them learn what they need to know about human bodies. They only become dangerous if a child is coerced into playing, if a child is physically or emotionally hurt, or if parents overreact with anger and punishment so that the child feels guilty and ashamed. Parents who encounter their children playing doctor, whether they perceive it to be harmful or not, should react calmly, ask the children to get dressed, and distract them with a snack or other play. Later, they can set some limits for their own child, if they wish. To children old enough to understand the concept of privacy, a parent might explain that although it is fine to want to see how other children look undressed, bodies are private. A parent might offer to find a book in the library with photographs or drawings of male and female bodies to help children satisfy their curiosity.

Preschool children enjoy touching their bodies, which some parents find disturbing. Although few of today's parents grew up with the old myths about masturbation (that it causes warts, hair on the palms, or failing eyesight, or that it means someone is a homosexual), some were exposed to an irrational emotional taboo. Now experts emphasize the benefits of masturbation. Men and women who have learned what gives them pleasure, they point out, are likely to have more fulfilling sexual experiences. Since masturbation relieves sexual tension, it lessens the pressure on adolescents to have sexual intercourse. Experts also warn that punishing or scolding children for doing something they know feels good may create an inner conflict that will interfere with their sexual development. Children can, however, understand that masturbation is something to be done in private.

Finally, the preschool years are not too early to begin encouraging children to break out of traditional sex roles. Parents can offer girls opportunities for physical activity, for example, and boys opportunities to play house. And they can encourage both girls and boys to be assertive as well as to express their emotions freely.

School Days (Ages 6 to 9)

Not until they are about five or six are most children curious about how babies get inside their mothers and then get out. Whatever explanation parents give should include the idea that intercourse is loving and caring. The Planned Parenthood manual offers one such explanation, which could be adjusted according to the age and interest of a child: ''When a husband and wife are loving each other in a special way, the man puts his penis in the woman's vagina and some fluid is released through the penis. There are many sperm cells in the fluid. If one of them meets an egg cell inside the mother, new life can begin to grow.''

In kindergarten and first grade, children often begin to use ''dirty'' words, though they may not know their meanings. Parents should calmly explain that these words are slang, and give them their proper names. Children also can be made to understand that it is impolite to use these words in public, and that some of them are insulting and demeaning.

According to Sigmund Freud, between the ages of about six and nine is a ''latency period,'' during which children repress their sexual feelings and fantasies as too dangerous; these do not emerge again until adolescence. Now it is widely believed instead that this is an age at which children have become aware of social attitudes about what is acceptable behavior and conversation, and this does not include sex. When their child is at this age, then, it may be up to parents to initiate discussions of sexual topics in order not to stem the flow of open communication.

Preteens (Ages 9 to 12)

During the preteen period, children experience the most profound physiological and psychological changes of their lifetimes. By the age of 10 they should be told what to expect, and by 12 they are mature enough for a full knowledge of intercourse and reproduction. Most children this age also need to be reassured that they are normal. One woman remembers stuffing her (unnecessary) first bra with tissues while another remembers trying to hide her unacceptably large breasts under a tight shirt. Many boys have suffered the dismay of having a body that compared unfavorably to others in the locker room. There is a wide variation in rates of normal development, and pubertal changes can take four to five years to complete for boys (after starting around age 11 or 12) and three to four years for girls (after starting anywhere from nine to 16 years of age).

Some experts consider these years to be the most critical time for sex education. Since many preteen children decide that they know it all, it is very important to dispel any myths they may have. This is also the last time when parents can discuss sexual matters factually and neutrally, because preteens do not yet relate the information to themselves. When parents discuss birth control or the risks and responsibilities of a sexual relationship at this age, there is less possibility of children confusing the *giving of information* with the *giving of permission*. Parents might say, ''We hope very much that you won't get sexually involved until you are mature enough to handle it—which is a long way off—but if you ever decide to, we hope you will use one of these kinds of birth control.''

Giving preteens correct information about sex will protect them later, when they might have accepted misinformation from a peer rather than admit ignorance.

Knowledgeable teens are less likely to be faced with situations that get out of hand or to be misled by popular misconceptions, such as "You can't get pregnant when you have your period" or "It's bad for a boy's health to get aroused and not be satisfied." Besides being given the facts of menstruation and ejaculation and the process of reproduction, children also need to be warned to avoid dangerous situations. They need to know, for instance, that drinking or using drugs impairs judgment and reduces sexual inhibitions.

Preteens also need to understand the moral and emotional aspects of sexuality. Parents can prepare children for adolescence by talking about the power of hormones and of peer pressure. They also can tell children that they will be attracted to many people before they are adults and that only relationships that are honest and equal are worth having. Parents may also want to discuss their own values or those of their religion concerning premarital sex.

In *Raising Your Child to Be a Sexually Healthy Adult*, coauthors John V. Flowers, Jennifer Horsman, and Bernard Schwartz encourage parents of preteens to help their children develop the skill of "limitation," the ability to define what they want to do and with whom. Even a young child can learn to state his limits and stand by them. If every playdate with a child's friend ends on a sour note because the child gets hurt wrestling, parents might suggest that he tell this friend the next time, "I would like to play with you. Maybe we could ride bikes or play checkers, but I don't want to wrestle anymore." With an older child it might be, "I'd like to hang out with you after school, but I don't like to play catch. Could we go bowling or something else instead?" Ideally, this will later translate for a teenage girl or boy into the ability to say to a date, "I want to kiss and hold hands but I don't want to make love with you now."

Adolescence (Ages 13 to 18)

Reading the statistics on teens and sex can be upsetting for parents. According to a survey of 14- to 21-year-olds published in *Seventeen* magazine (October 1989), 24 percent had intercourse by the age of 15 and 60 percent by the age of 18. Yet these same statistics also tell parents and their children that not "everybody" is doing it. Even among those who are no longer virgins, according to Robert C. Kolodny, M.D., and his coauthors in *How to Survive Your Adolescent's Adolescence*, many do not have intercourse frequently. Most have sex with only one partner over a period of time, and some have intercourse as an experiment and then go for long stretches of time before doing it again.

There are other upsetting statistics, however. The teenage pregnancy rate in the United States is shockingly high, more than twice that of Canada, France, Sweden, and England. Each year more than a million American teenagers become pregnant, most unintentionally. And according to recent government statistics, 2.5 million teenagers have sexually transmitted diseases, not including AIDS. These diseases include gonorrhea, herpes, syphilis, venereal disease, and chlamydia (a bacterial infection that can infect both men and women and cause pelvic inflammatory disease, sterility, eye infections, and blindness).

Sadly, many adolescents are not mature enough intellectually or emotionally to handle a sexual relationship. They can do harm to themselves or their partners. According to Carol Cassell, Ph.D., a former president of the American Association of Sex Educators, Counselors, and Therapists, in *Straight from the Heart*, before teenagers enter a sexual relationship they need to "have developed a personal sense of self-esteem and ability to communicate with another person about this person's as well as their own intimacy needs

171

and feelings, and they should also be ready to be responsible about contraception.''

Parents can convey to their children the belief that sex is one of the most profound experiences people can share. They can communicate that making love requires a decision and entails a responsibility. They can stress that it should not happen just because of an impulse, as many teenagers claim it does. There are options other than intercourse for relieving sexual tension that parents can suggest, such as masturbation and physical activities, including sports. Parents can reassure their children that they are perfectly normal if they want to say no. Adolescents should understand that it is wrong to use sex as a test of love (''If you love me, you would . . .'') and that anyone who tries to force another person into having sex is being exploitative.

Parents should also talk frankly with teenagers about the consequences of sex without protection. Besides discussing the threat of contracting a potentially fatal disease, they should describe the physical and emotional dangers of being or getting someone pregnant and the responsibilities of raising a baby. Many teenagers romanticize the love a baby will bring into their lives and imagine that they will gain status among their peers. In fact, babies demand a great deal of care and patience, and unmarried teenage parents are suddenly thrust into adulthood before they are ready. They are likely to drop out of school, and without education or training, their chances of being able to support a baby are slim. The baby often becomes a burden on the teens' parents or relatives, creating family tensions. Often teenage fathers are denied any parental role by the mother's family and possibly the mother herself because of their anger toward him and their shame about the pregnancy. Teenagers who accuse their parents of being alarmist on this subject and so dismiss their warnings may be persuaded by printed material from agencies that help pregnant teenagers or by talking to a teenage parent.

Adolescents need all this information and they *want* it. In polls, according to the Planned Parenthood manual, nine out of 10 teenagers say that they want to get information about sex from their parents. Yet only about one in 10 does. In some families, parents' communication with their teenagers is limited to trying to control their behavior.

It is unrealistic for parents to assume that their adolescent children will not have sexual relationships without their approval. Parents can, however, set limits on what they allow in their own homes. By being clear about expectations, even strict in a caring way, they can also give children a sense of security. Teenagers may use parental limits and prohibitions to fall back on if they need support for decisions that may not be popular with their peers. More important, parents can convey the message that no matter what their children do, they will continue to love them. With this knowledge, children will feel free to come to them with their feelings and conflicts.

Fortunately, for parents who want to raise sexually healthy children, comfortable with their sexuality but also responsible and moral in their sexual choices, teaching them about sex is not an isolated lesson. Children will bring to their sexual relationships the values they learned growing up, including a sense of their own worth and how to treat others.

CHAPTER EIGHT

• • • • • •

What's New About Drugs?

Liz is the oldest of our four daughters. She was 16 years old when we found out that she was chemically dependent, but it had probably been going on for a couple of years.

About a year before the crisis, we began to have nagging suspicions that she might be using drugs. Small, insignificant changes occurred, and taken one at a time they pointed to nothing more than teenage behavior. We also suspected she was taking money from us, but we couldn't prove it. I did have her checked by our family doctor under the guise of a routine physical. The results were all negative and the diagnosis was that she was a "normal teenager."

In hindsight I realize that she was going through withdrawal the summer before we knew she was addicted. She spent an entire weekend on the living room sofa, throwing up and swearing at us. But I had no idea then what withdrawal looked like. And I was heavily into denial at the time.

A few months later, I went into her room to get a book she had forgotten to take to school. When I think about the evidence of drug and alcohol use I found there, I can still feel some of the rage inside me. That night, I confronted her. I screamed about it being illegal and how terrible the effects were. When I asked her why such an intelligent, logical kid would do something so stupid, her answer was, "I like it." She admitted that she was a user, but she would not admit that she had a problem.

I talked to someone in the drug program at Liz's school,

who told me that first she needed to be assessed. I didn't give her any choice about going. I feared she would hate me for what I was doing. I also feared she had already suffered some lasting adverse effects. We found out that she was in middle- to late-stage three of alcohol and drug dependency. She had been using marijuana, cocaine, and alcohol for over a year. She had blacked out eight or nine times, tried to quit by herself two or three times, and had barely escaped being picked up by the police many times. They suggested she go into residential treatment immediately.

My husband was in shock, denying the severity of the problem despite the facts. I felt a lot of guilt as a parent. I am terrified of drugs, and I was always talking to my kids about them. I used TV commercials for drugs to explain that you don't take pills for everything. We also talked about alcohol. I did the best that I knew how to do at the time, and I don't think anything else I could have done would have made a difference, short of following Liz everywhere. (And that would have made her rebel more.)

When we visited Liz in the Adolescent Residential Treatment Program several days later, she was beginning to look so much better—healthy and bright-faced. The changes she had undergone before we brought her to treatment were so small and widely spaced that we didn't notice them until she was recovering. As I began to see our beautiful, thoughtful, caring Liz again, I realized she had become a selfish, demanding, verbally abusive kid with bloodshot eyes.

When she came home, we all walked around on eggshells for a long time. I realized what a relief it had been not having to deal with her on a daily basis. She was now rational and logical, but I could still recall all the pretreatment incidents.

The months went by and I watched her choose to give up

all her user friends, struggle to make up her schoolwork, regularly attend support meetings, and make her daily choice to remain clean and sober. But the statistics on relapse for teenagers are terrible. I waited for the other shoe to drop. A year later it did.

As recommended by the treatment center, we had house rules that you couldn't live at home if you were using drugs. So I told her to leave. She could come back if she had a clean urine test. It was the hardest thing I've ever done in my whole life. She went to live with friends and came back just before school started with a clean test. She hasn't used drugs since.

Now, five years later, she is fine. She graduated from high school, went on to college, and recently married. But she will be a potential addict for the rest of her life. I will be standing on the sidelines, ever watchful and ready to help. But she is the only one who can choose her sobriety.

I still talk to my three younger daughters about it all the time. It's part of our everyday conversation. They tell me about kids they know who are taking drugs. We talk about parents of kids they know who drink or take pills or drugs. After seeing what their sister went through, they are all committed to not using drugs. I just hope they stay committed.

—A MOTHER

In Lebanon, Pennsylvania, in 1989, police officers discovered a group of children selling bags of lawn clippings and bags of sugar at a make-believe drug stand—horrifying, but not unbelievable. Drugs, after all, are commonplace for many children today, as they never were for their parents. In New York City small children have arrived at school wearing beepers linked to real-life drug dealers.

In the 1940s, according to a listing by the Fullerton, California, Police Department and the California Department of Education, the three leading discipline problems in schools were talking, chewing gum, and making noise. In the 1980s they were drug abuse, alcohol abuse, and pregnancy. In 1962 less than 4 percent of the population had experimented with illegal drugs. By the 1980s up to 57 percent had experimented before graduating from high school. The drugs, too, have changed. Today's marijuana, for instance, is 10 times stronger on the average than what was available in the 1960s, and the cocaine is much purer and, thus, more potent. Children also have easier access to drugs and alcohol. They get them from their friends, older brothers and sisters, and, with false IDs, from liquor stores. Some children filch from well-stocked family liquor cabinets and medicine chests. Some buy over-the-counter drugs and other addictive items: caffeine pills or diet pills, antihistamines, cough medicine with a high alcohol content, nasal inhalers, typewriter correction fluid, lighter fluid, and aerosol cans.

Ironically, the first drugs to sweep the nation were the ''wonder drugs'' of the 1940s and 1950s: antibiotics, tranquilizers, and steroids. The underside of this medical miracle was the newborn habit of pill-popping and the popular notion that pills could solve every problem. Drug abuse then, however, was perceived mostly as the problem of the urban poor. It was only in the mid- to late 1960s that it became a national concern. Drugs were an emblem of the youthful counterculture, the free-spirited and rebellious, fed up with the adult world in general and the Vietnam War in particular. In the 1970s, drug use, especially of marijuana and cocaine, became almost respectable among college students and young professionals.

The Drugs of Today

Today drugs and alcohol are used all over the country by adolescents of all social classes. Drug use by young people dropped in 1989 to the lowest level since 1975, the year when anthropologist Lloyd Johnston, Ph.D., at the University of Michigan's Institute for Social Research, began taking an annual survey of high school seniors. But it is still higher in the United States than in any other industrialized nation. In addition, life expectancy has increased for every age group in the country over the last 30 years—except for 16- to 24-year-olds. Three-quarters of the deaths of these young people are caused by injuries, suicides, and homicides, a large proportion of which are related to drug and alcohol use.

Of the students surveyed by Dr. Johnston in 1989 (who do not include high school dropouts), about 51 percent reported trying an illegal drug before graduating from high school, 17 percent reported current marijuana use (within the last 30 days), 2.8 percent reported current cocaine use, and 1.4 percent current crack use. According to Dr. Johnston, however, other information indicates that the crack problem is worse than these figures suggest. As for alcohol abuse, Dr. Johnston has called it a "cause for renewed concern." Most of those students surveyed in 1989 reported drinking alcohol, and 60 percent had had at least one drink in the last 30 days.

But the exposure to legal and illegal drugs begins long before high school. Almost one-third of the fourth graders responding to a Weekly Reader Periodicals national survey said that they had been pressured by their peers to try alcohol and marijuana. For sixth graders the figure is 40 percent. Meanwhile, the average age of first use of drugs or alcohol is about 12 and is continuing to drop. By the age of

13, 30 percent of boys and 22 percent of girls consider themselves drinkers, according to *Drug-Free Communities,* a publication from the Federal Office for Substance Abuse Prevention. It concludes, "Research confirms that the earlier kids begin to use, the more likely they are to continue—and to escalate—their drug use."

Who Gets Hooked?

There is no single reason why children, or adults, become addicted. A cluster of factors, internal and external, can lead someone to be attracted to or become dependent on drugs or alcohol.

Among the internal factors, the nature of adolescence itself poses a risk. This is an age when it is normal and healthy for young people to experiment with different behaviors and to rebel against parental expectations in order to establish a separate identity. One mother whose teenage daughters' purplish-white hair outraged their relatives at a wake said, "Given the alternatives, if this is the way they choose to rebel, I am thrilled." It is also an age of self-consciousness and conformity with one's peers. Inevitably, the influence over teenagers shifts away from their parents and toward others their own age. In addition to these factors is adolescents' exaggerated sense of their own invincibility, which may lead to acting dangerously.

Some people are also biologically prone to becoming addicted, perhaps because of some hereditary aspect of their brain metabolism. The sons and daughters of alcoholics, for instance, are three to four times more likely to become dependent on alcohol than are children of nonalcoholics. Parents should make sure their children know about this, in the same way they would alert them to any other aspect of their family health history.

Because drugs and alcohol are often used to mute sadness or to escape from frightening situations, certain children are more at risk than others. Children suffering through their parents' painful divorce or other trauma, or those with behavior or learning problems, for example, may be tempted by drugs, which make them feel happier, more capable, or less inhibited, though the effect is only temporary. Children who are bored or spend a great deal of time alone without adult supervision also may turn to drugs or alcohol because of peer pressure. Help with all of these kinds of problems cannot guarantee that children will stay drug-free, but it will at least provide an alternative.

Some children are attracted to drugs and alcohol by their image in the media. Many advertisers promote the take-a-pill solution to problems. In addition, children are exposed regularly to portraits of drug users as sophisticated and cool. For example, some rock songs sanction drug and alcohol use, while in ads for alcohol, drinking is associated with success and sex appeal. Even sporting events are often sponsored by alcohol and cigarette companies.

Recently the television networks (though still not the movies) have made some steps toward change. They are donating airtime to broadcast antidrug messages and have adopted formal or informal guidelines to avoid glorifying drug use on their programs. Guidelines for NBC shows, for example, state that every drug-related criminal has to suffer serious consequences, according to Rosalyn Weinman, vice president for program standards and community relations (*New York Times*, November 12, 1989). Many television, movie, and rock stars have also joined campaigns against drug use.

The major external pressure on preteens and teenagers, and even on younger children, comes from peers. Some children lack the strength to resist friends who encourage them to try drugs or alcohol or who taunt them for refusing. For them, the need to be one of the gang may just be too strong a pull. They may have low self-esteem or may never have developed good decision-making skills. Fortunately, not all teenage groups revolve around drugs and alcohol. And even the disturbing statistics on drug and alcohol use do not prove that "everyone" is doing it. In fact, it is quite the reverse.

All the blame, however, does not fall on society and other teenagers. Parents themselves are important role models for their children's drug behavior. No matter how rebellious they may seem, children normally try to be like their parents because they want parents' approval. According to a family study published by the Pacific Institute for Research and Evaluation, children are more prone to drug abuse if their parents smoke cigarettes; abuse alcohol or are alcoholics; take illicit drugs; use any substance for stress; or convey an ambivalent or positive attitude toward drugs.

Children watch how their parents deal with stress and how they have fun. Parents who come home from work and immediately head for the liquor cabinet are sending a message to their children. Parents who install "fuzz-busters" in their cars to cheat on the speed limit may find it hard to punish a child for cheating on the legal drinking age. And those parents who abuse drugs themselves (even prescription drugs, such as tranquilizers and diet pills) have less credibility when they take a stand against their children's behavior. Parents should think twice before asking a child to bring them a beer from the refrigerator, to light their cigarette, or to get a bottle of aspirin or some other drug from the medicine cabinet.

One father, whose oldest son recently returned from a drug-treatment program, decided to deal with an addiction of his own. "I have quit smoking as of two months ago. I promised the children I would not smoke in the house, and

I have not.'' To see him struggle and succeed will be a powerful, positive message to his family.

Parents do not, however, have to become teetotalers in order to keep their children off drugs or alcohol. An adolescent can understand and accept that mature adults can handle certain experiences that young people cannot. They can also understand the difference between having a glass of wine or beer and using alcohol as a narcotic for emotional pain. Adults who use legal drugs responsibly and do not use alcohol routinely provide a good example of wise moderation for their children's future behavior.

Prevention

Although federal legislation from 1986 mandates programs from kindergarten through the twelfth grade, the quality of drug education in the United States varies from state to state and from one school district to another. Thus, parents cannot count on the schools to do all the work.

Drug education at home should not begin when a teenager comes home high from a party. It can begin with a three-year-old, when parents talk abut nutrition or warn him against poisons. Whenever parents use medicine, they can explain how important it is to follow the directions and read the precautions. They can explain that prescription medicines are intended for a specific person with a specific need and that children should never take medicine without their permission. Old prescriptions that are no longer needed should be thrown out, and parents should use even over-the-counter medicine, such as aspirin or vitamins, only for legitimate reasons. It is important to avoid giving the message that taking a pill will solve life's problems.

Parents can lay the groundwork for prevention by fostering honesty and communication within the family on all subjects. They should try not to be too judgmental and critical, dispensing only dos and don'ts, lest children become hesitant to bring up serious issues about which they have conflicting feelings. Children should know that drinking, smoking, and drugs are subjects they can always discuss with their parents.

By the time children are in the fifth grade, parents should begin talking specifically about alcohol and illegal drugs. Children this age already may be feeling pressure from their peers, but the pendulum of influence is still on the parents' side. Parents could ask, "Do any of your friends or other kids in your school use drugs?" Or they could discuss an incident on a television program or in the news about a drunk-driving accident or a celebrity who has gotten into trouble because of drugs or alcohol. If parents feel comfortable, they might want to talk about their own past experience, but they should be careful not to make it sound as if drinking or taking drugs is normal behavior and part of growing up. Nor should these discussions consist of merely relating horror stories, because scare tactics usually do not work. Children tend to feel immortal and resist believing that anything terrible could happen to them. Besides, they have seen that celebrities who are arrested for drugs recover and return to high-paying jobs. They also may have friends who use drugs and alcohol and seem unaffected.

Before parents talk to their children, they should be sure of their own values and feelings about drug abuse. Do they believe, for instance, that recreational use of marijuana and alcohol is acceptable? Can they define *responsible* use of drugs and alcohol? Many experts believe that for children, any use of chemical substances is abuse because drugs are just too damaging to development physically, intellectually, and socially.

Parents need to communicate clearly and firmly their values and beliefs. "Even though I was horrified about the idea of drugs," said one mother whose son was treated for drug abuse, "I didn't really tell him what I expected. I was too liberal and loosey-goosey because I didn't think it was my problem. We said, 'We expect you to be responsible and take care of your body and not abuse chemicals. And come to us if you have any problems.' But that wasn't clear enough. And we were too relaxed about overnights; I didn't always call to make sure a parent was home." Some parents acknowledge to their older children that there are levels of experimentation and that having a beer at a friend's house is obviously less risky than buying street drugs. But they need to emphasize that even such forms of low-risk behavior in the area of drugs and alcohol are not desirable.

In *Saying No Is Not Enough*, psychologist Robert Schwebel, Ph.D., suggests the kind of clear message a parent might give: "The reason I don't think children should use alcohol or other drugs is because this is a time for you . . . to learn how to cope with stress and how to solve problems, without drugs. It's a time to learn how to make good relationships, without drugs. If you get high on drugs, it can keep you from developing your own inner strength. Anyway, drugs are powerful substances and can be harmful. As you know, even adults make poor decisions about drug use and can't control themselves. I think the risks are much greater for young people. And drugs are illegal. I don't want you to break the law." Most parents would add that no time, including adulthood, is appropriate for using drugs or alcohol as a substitute for dealing with life's sorrows and joys.

Once parents have declared their policy on drugs and alcohol, they should set some family rules and clear consequences for breaking them. One couple grounded their daughter for two weeks when she arrived home drunk from her first high school party. "I can't swear that she has never experimented since and gotten away with it,'' her mother said, ''but at least she knows exactly how we feel about it.''

Family rules can also give a child an easy way out of a situation he doesn't quite dare to confront head-on. ''No, thanks,'' he might say when friends pressure him. ''My parents told me I would have to wait a whole extra year to get my driver's license if they caught me messing around with drugs.''

Besides having their feelings and expectations straight, parents need to have their information straight, too. When they raise the issue of drugs and alcohol, they should know more than their children do. They should also be able to explain the legal consequences of drug use. Fortunately information is easily available. There are many books on the subject in libraries and bookstores, and the federal government publishes useful up-to-date booklets, which can be ordered free. (Write to: National Clearinghouse for Alcohol and Drug Information, Information Services, P.O. Box 2345, Rockville, MD 20852, or call: (301) 468-2600 and ask for a publications catalog.)

Before beginning a discussion, parents should try to assess just how much their children already know and what misconceptions they may have by listening to what they say about drugs and their feelings about them. Then parents should be careful not to overreact. They also should not try to deny the pleasurable effects of drugs. Instead, they should emphasize the dangerous physical and psychological effects. They might even take a teenager to an open meeting at a nearby drug or alcohol rehabilitation program. The dangers of drug abuse are real; there is no need for parents to exaggerate and lose their credibility. Even young children can understand drug dependence. Dr. Schwebel explains it this way: ''Some people take drugs to feel good. But if this is the only way they know how to make themselves feel good, then they will *depend* on the drugs. They will *need* them to feel good. Their whole life will center around drugs and nothing else. In extreme cases, they'll forget about their jobs and family. The drugs will control them.''

The greatest risk from drugs, of course, is death, not only from overdose but also from accidents related to drug or alcohol use. Alcohol and/or cocaine use is a factor in many car accidents in this country. And nearly half the young people who commit suicide had been involved with alcohol or drugs, about 30 percent having been drunk or high at the time. Children need to know that marijuana and alcohol will weaken their reflexes and that drugs can also heighten emotions to frightening proportions.

Although children often have difficulty thinking about the long-term effects of their actions, these particular dangers will strike home for most teenagers. Almost every high school bears the sad memory of a student who took his own life or who was killed in a car accident because of drunk driving.

''I know a lot of people think it's a heavy burden to lay on young kids,'' said the father of a recovering drug-addicted teenager and an advocate for early drug education in school, ''but this problem is not going to go away if you close your eyes.''

Life Skills Training

The most successful approaches to drug-abuse prevention provide more than information. They develop personal qualities in children that can help them resist drugs. The goal is to build their self-esteem and strengthen their ability to make sound judgments, to resist pressure from friends, and to meet needs that would otherwise be met by drugs.

Many experts believe that children who grow up with a firm sense of self-esteem and strong family ties are least likely to become involved with drugs and alcohol. Parents can encourage these positive feelings in a number of ways (some of which are described in chapters 7 and 9). Most important is to value a child's individuality. Parents should support their children's special interests. They should give them opportunities to enjoy success and give them increasing rights and responsibilities as they grow up. It is also important for children to learn how to pick themselves up after a loss, whether it be in a game or a friendship. Children who are consistently protected from the normal pains of living may, at the first sign of adversity, look for the easy way out. Finally, parents should encourage their children to take pride in their differentness. "You don't have to do everything just like your friends if you don't want to," parents might say. "In the long run, they will respect you more for sticking to what you believe." They might also point out that true friends will not force you to do something against your principles.

Children learn problem-solving skills through practice. They should know the reasoning behind family rules and as often as possible participate in setting those rules that affect their lives. Parents should discuss why people take risks, which risks might be good ones, and which ones might be foolish. And they should always point out the values reflected by different points of view.

Some children turn to drugs because they are bored. Parents should be alert to this problem and help their children find enriching activities to fill their time: arts programs; sports; academic activities; a part-time job; or volunteer work at hospitals, nursing homes, museums, or libraries. Boy Scouts, Girl Scouts, and other clubs also provide social and educational activities. One mother credits a YMCA swim team with keeping her child drug-free through high school. "Andy likes sports more than anything; swimming especially is important in his life. And you can't smoke and swim." Once children discover an interest, parents should bolster it by attending their recitals or competitions, admiring what they have done or made, or just asking how their hobby is going.

Even with all this support, it is very difficult to resist peer pressure. Parents need to give their children practical tools to deal with everyday problems and encourage them to stay away from people who use drugs and the places they frequent. If children are being pressured to use drugs, parents can tell them to find a group of nonusers and take a stand or walk away together. Children may also feel more confident if they have learned certain responses, such as these lines recommended by journalist Geraldine Youcha and Judith S. Seixas, an alcoholism counselor, in their book, *Drugs, Alcohol, and Your Children:*

"No thanks. I've got too much to do today."

". . . I've got to be with it for basketball practice."

". . . I just end up embarrassing myself."

". . . I don't want to fry my brains."

". . . My parents told me I would be grounded for three weeks, and I don't want to take the chance of missing my friend's party."

Sometimes reverse peer pressure works: "It's too boring to get stoned. I can't believe you really want to do that."

Parents should also offer their children a way to get out of a fix: by coming to them. "If you're ever anywhere and it looks as if you're in trouble or it's a bad situation," one father told his 16-year-old son, "call us and we will come get you." Parents must be sure, however, that when that call comes, before discussing whatever the "trouble" was, they praise their child for making the right decision.

It is unrealistic to expect children never to experiment with drugs and alcohol. But if parents provide love and as much prevention as possible, set a clear, firm standard of behavior, and consistently act according to it themselves, they can reasonably hope that their children will have enough inner strength not to let experimentation turn into use.

Gateway Drugs

Another aspect of drug abuse prevention is the concept of "gateway drugs." The use of these drugs—tobacco, alcohol, and marijuana—in early adolescence is highly correlated with later use of such drugs as cocaine, amphetamines, tranquilizers, PCP, heroin, and LSD. Youcha and Seixas describe a typical progression from beer to wine to cigarettes or hard liquor, then marijuana and finally other illicit drugs. They point out that crack (smokable cocaine) is an exception, attracting young people with little or no other experience with drugs.

Although many of today's parents grew up thinking of cigarettes as an innocent emblem of adulthood, by now tobacco is known to be a dangerous and addictive drug. Dr. Lloyd Johnston, of the University of Michigan's Institute for Social Research, has pointed out that cigarettes will kill more of today's teenagers than all other drugs combined. The United States Office of Smoking and Health estimates that today one in five teenagers smoke. Although peer pressure is usually cited as the main reason for starting, parents who smoke are also a major influence.

Alcohol, the drug used by the greatest number of teenagers, is also the drug that worries adults least because it is the most familiar. But the dangers of alcohol to health are serious, and young people are more vulnerable than adults. They also become dependent more easily. Added to this is the danger of combining alcohol and driving. According to a Gallup poll, one-third of all teenagers admit to having been in a car with a driver their age who had been drinking or using drugs.

Some of today's parents associate marijuana with their youth and with the notion at that time that it was harmless. They may know many people who tried or used marijuana then and never went on to other drugs. But the marijuana sold on the streets today contains 10 times the amount of tetrahydrocannabinol (THC), its psychedelic chemical, than that which was sold in the 1960s. According to the American Academy of Pediatrics, ''Marijuana can be harmful to the physical and psychosocial health and development of children and adolescents.'' Furthermore, the use of marijuana introduces children into a world of drug users.

Informing children about gateway drugs, then, is an important step in preventing drug abuse. Some parents worry that this information will plant ideas in their children's minds. But instead, like information about sex, it gives them a basis for making responsible decisions and decreases the risk that they will give in to pressure, temptation, or curiosity.

Treating a Drug Problem

Parents frequently fail to recognize signs indicating that their children are using drugs. They may simply overlook them, like the mother earlier in this chapter, who assumed it was not her problem. Or they may turn away out of fear that their child's drug use means that they have failed as parents. Some parents become "enablers," covering up for their children, making excuses, sparing them the consequences of their behavior. While covering up for a child's problem is often rooted in love, this practice does much more harm than good.

The best way for parents to head off a drug problem is to keep an active interest in their children's lives so that they will notice changes in behavior or friendships that could signal a problem. Parents should get to know their children's friends. They can encourage their children to invite them home or they can volunteer to chaperon or sponsor their children's group activities. Parents should also keep their eyes and ears open—read the school newspaper, look at the yearbook, talk to their children's friends—but not snoop unless they have reason to be suspicious. Parents should show respect for their children's privacy and their need for time alone with their friends. Regular communication with other parents can provide information about children's activities and community standards of what is acceptable behavior (a good counter to the "Everybody else gets to . . ." argument). Parents can also work together to arrange safe, interesting activities for children, especially after school and during vacations.

Some common warning signs of drug and alcohol abuse are a new set of friends, a decline in grades, dropping out of activities enjoyed in the past, refusal to participate in family events, deterioration in appearance, irritability, secretive phone calls, solitariness, lying, and the disappearance of money or pills or other medicine. There are also symptoms related to particular substances, which are described in books and pamphlets about drug abuse.

A pamphlet from the U.S. Office for Substance Abuse Prevention, *What You Can Do About Drug Use in America*, describes four stages of alcohol and other drug abuse:

During Stage 1, experimentation, there may be no visible behavior changes.

Stage 2 is characterized by more frequent use. Users actively seek the effects of the drug, and its use may extend beyond the weekends. They may have found a regular source and a new group of friends. Signs may include experiencing a lack of motivation and having trouble with school.

By Stage 3, users desire the effects of the drug intensely and are using it daily. There may be trouble at home and with the law.

At Stage 4, the user needs increasing amounts of the drug just to feel normal. Physical signs may include a cough, sore throat, loss of weight, or exhaustion. By now family life may be suffering and users may be resorting to crime to get money for their drugs.

If parents notice any of these symptoms, they should first express their concern about the specific behaviors and about their child's well-being. Only if their child's response warrants it should they broach the subject of possible drug use. If the child is abusing drugs, they should try to wait until he is no longer high to confront him, then avoid an angry outburst, which will only cut off communication. The next step is to find out what drug or drugs he is using, how often, where he got them, and, if possible, why he thinks he is doing it. The problem may be worse than he is willing to admit, even to himself. Parents should continue to express their concern not only about the drug use but also about whatever other problems the child may be having.

If a child's drug use is at a low level, he may accept his parents' arguments against drugs and agree to stop. Nevertheless, parents will have to be vigilant. On the other hand, if the child continues to use drugs without considering the effects, including the danger to himself and others, and is unwilling to give them up, parents will need to get professional help quickly. Referrals can be obtained from the school, a member of the clergy, a doctor, a social worker, a psychologist, Alcoholics Anonymous or Narcotics Anonymous, or by looking in the *Yellow Pages* under "Alcoholism Treatment" or "Drug Abuse Information and Treatment." Before parents choose any professionals to treat their child, they should meet with them and discuss their points of view.

The first step in treating a drug problem is usually an assessment, which includes a complete physical, psychological tests, and a history of drug use. Then detoxification is necessary. Treatment choices for drug abusers are drug-free outpatient care (usually four to six months), short-term in-patient care (four to six weeks), and a therapeutic community (six to 24 months). When treatment is over, most programs require regular attendance at self-help groups, such as Alcoholics Anonymous.

It is very important to choose a good program. "The thing I found scary," said a mother who attended a family program at the hospital where her daughter was being treated, "was to hear other parents talk about how awful other treatment places were. It's horrible to be at the mercy of someone who's treating your kid. How do you know which treatment is good and which isn't? You don't know, if it's your first experience with such a problem."

Experts provide some guidelines parents can use in choosing professional help. Most experts recommend that programs require family involvement, which improves the chances of recovery by a factor of 10, according to research by the National Federation of Parents for Drug Free Youth. In *When Saying No Isn't Enough*, Ken Barun, former head of the Cenikor Foundation, which specializes in drug- and alcohol-abuse rehabilitation, and writer Philip Bashe list these other important qualities of a good program:

- State license or approval for the facility and its academic program, or accreditation by the Joint Commission on Accreditation of Hospitals
- Detoxification on-site or in a nearby hospital
- A policy of total abstinence
- A counselor-to-client ratio of at most 1:10; about half the counselors should be former drug abusers, and most should be certified
- A physician and a doctorate-level mental health professional available at all times
- Affiliation with a nearby hospital
- Therapy groups for girls only (they are often outnumbered by boys 10:1 in treatment)
- Weekly urine tests for outpatients
- Aftercare as part of the program, either on-site or through Alcoholics Anonymous or a similar self-help group
- A recovery rate of at least 67 percent

Finally, parents need to be proud, not ashamed, that their child is going for help, no matter what the neighbors think, so that he will feel proud, too. Parents also need to continue to convey their love. "When Liz got the graduation medallion from her program," said the mother whose story begins this chapter, "one of the things she said was a huge thanks to me for never giving up on her and never ceasing to let her know where I was and what I believed in and that I loved her. She said that my belief in her, though she was clouded with the drugs and alcohol, always managed to shine through and gave her a goal while she was in treatment. Knowing just how much she was loved made her journey a lot easier because she knew she was never alone."

CHAPTER NINE

. . . . . .

Creating Family Networks

When I was growing up, we always did a lot with my father's family. My grandmother was very much a force in our lives. Some of her brothers lived with her and all of the nieces and nephews and cousins would stay with her whenever they came into town. We had dinner with them every Sunday.

A major difference in my kids' lives is that we live so far away from any relatives. If my family was nearby we would get together often, but they're in Michigan and we're in New York. My kids have gotten to know their aunts and uncles and cousins, but it's work and it's always a trek. We go out to visit twice a year, at Christmas and in June, and my relatives visit us. Before my parents got too old, they would visit us about twice a year, for a birthday or a holiday. I call my mother once or twice a week, and I have contact with my sisters throughout the year, even though they live far away. More information passes through my mother.

My husband's family isn't close, but I think it's important to keep the connection. I push him to call his parents so that the kids can talk to them. We also visit them on the trips when we visit my family.

Another difference for my children is that where I grew up the magnet of the neighborhood was the church. But I've been away from my religion for 10 years or so. We've tried to create another kind of community with friends. When your kids are in play groups and nursery school, you can make good friendships without having to do a lot of work. My husband and a friend from that time still run a baseball game every Sunday in the summer. They draw in a lot of kids and parents. We also have a community in our apartment building. All the families with kids became friendly, and I think the kids really rely on one another. We started out having dinner together sometimes and celebrating the kids' birthdays, and it just grew. If something happened to either my husband or me—one of us was sick or laid up or in the hospital—these people would be there to help us.

These relationships are harder to create and maintain than family. With relatives, you have occasions when you all get together. With friends, you have to make them. It's really nice to establish some traditions with friends. The advantage of friends is that you can pick and choose; with relatives you can't. I do worry sometimes who are going to be the anchors for my kids, who are going to be the people they will relate to like I relate to my relatives.

—A MOTHER

Because we moved a great deal with my husband's job, I was separated from my oldest daughter soon after she had her first child and from my second daughter after she entered college. I was able to see my grandchildren only once or twice a year. Of course, I wrote letters all the time and called frequently. But I really missed so much of their growing up.

After my husband died, I began hopping on airplanes every chance I got to go see my scattered family. Finally, my oldest daughter persuaded me to move near them. I am now within a few miles of all but two of my great-grandchildren. I have my own apartment, but I see almost everyone at least once a week. And I go to all the baseball games, concerts, and birthday parties. My great-grandchildren are all so different; it's fun to see them change and grow. But I still wish I could see the other children more frequently. I now have a step-

*grandson that I haven't had much of a chance to get to know.
I can't travel much anymore, so my phone bills are high.*

—A GREAT-GRANDMOTHER

*I was never very close to most of my family, so I created
a family from my friends. These are people I have known for
years. We depend on each other and are always there for each
other. Now that I have a daughter, these friendships have
become even stronger. Karen has many 'aunts' and 'uncles'
whom she sees frequently. Both of my parents passed away
several years ago. My older sister, the one relative I feel close
to, has taken on somewhat the role of grandmother to Karen.
She really spoils Karen when we visit her on the weekends.
We also know a few older people who live in my apartment
building, so Karen is often grandmothered and grandfa-
thered.*

—A SINGLE MOTHER

Fragmented, *isolated,* and *insular*—these are adjectives
some commentators attach to the modern American
family. Families undeniably have shrunk in recent times,
and many have moved far away from their hometowns and
relatives. In some others, parents and children have been
so busy with their own friends, careers, and activities that
they have lost touch with their extended families. Nevertheless, social scientists are beginning to note a rediscovery
of family connections as a valuable resource in a fast-
changing, increasingly impersonal world. In a December 3,
1989, article in the *Des Moines Register*, Timothy H. Bru-
baker, director of the Family and Child Study Center at
Miami University in Oxford, Ohio, said in an interview,
"We're just starting to notice that we need more than buying a four-bedroom house and a BMW. In the '90s, I see
the upwardly mobile groups viewing intimate family relationships as more positive."

Not all aspects of modern life are forces pulling families apart. Some actually have helped to keep them together. Modern medicine, for instance, has increased life expectancy so that older generations live longer and healthier lives than ever before. In 1890 the typical mother did not live to see her youngest child marry. Now the typical mother is likely to have one-third of her life still in front of her when her last child is gone. Many of today's children can look forward to knowing their great-grandchildren. Modern technology provides easy access to long-distance travel and communication that was once inconceivable. Although sometimes it requires ''work'' and it can be ''a trek'' (as one of the mothers was quoted as saying at the beginning of this chapter), it is still possible to create networks of relatives, neighbors, and friends, and to maintain a strong family unit.

Families on the Move

Physical distance between family members can easily lead to emotional distance, and mobility often contributes to the fragmentation of families. According to statistics collected yearly by the United States Bureau of the Census, the rate of moving in 1987 for children aged 1 to 4 was 26.7 percent; for children 5 to 9 the rate was 19.9 percent; and for 10- to 14-year-olds the rate was 16.1 percent. Yet Americans have been on the move for much of their history. The rates for 1949–50 were not much different from those of today. Even in the 1800s many immigrants moved away from the East Coast soon after they arrived, and wagon trains carried other families farther west. These immigrants, however, usually were moving to join relatives or countrymen who had already settled in certain regions. Unrelated families in wagon trains heading for the same destination often forged bonds as they traveled and built homes near each other in small frontier towns. But modern moves, often dictated by job changes, divorces, or marriages, may take families vast distances from relatives and old friends.

Even a short move within the same area is unsettling for both children and adults, wrenching them from a web of familiar faces and places. For children especially, their temperament and age can make a move more or less stressful. While some children by nature adjust well to change, most children prefer stability, especially at the stages when they are making developmental strides, testing their independence, and forging important friendships. Moves are often particularly upsetting for children in their early to mid-teens, since at this age they are worried about being accepted into a peer group. One 13-year-old girl, whose family moved a quarter mile away to a different school district, informed her parents fiercely, ''You are ruining my whole life!''

Though a move may be unavoidable, parents can make the transition easier by planning ahead. Many experts recommend waiting to move until the school year is over. A summer move gives the whole family some time to get to know the neighborhood before school begins. Parents may be able to visit the school with their children and ask about any summer assignments or academic requirements that may be different from those at the former school. They may also be able to arrange for their children to meet classmates who live nearby. And many children feel less conspicuous as newcomers on the first day of school before friendships and cliques have solidified.

On the other hand, agencies that help corporations move the families of their employees have found that many prefer moving during the school year. They report that these children tend to be given special treatment at school instead of perhaps being lost in the shuffle at the beginning of the year.

Once the move has been announced, some children withdraw or act uninterested; others become angry at the disruption of their lives. Parents can help children adjust by explaining exactly what will be happening and when, and by encouraging them to participate in the packing, especially of their own belongings. They should show them pictures of the new house and new neighborhood and, if possible, take them to visit.

Parents should also give their children a chance to say good-bye to the old house and neighborhood. Some parents throw a going-away party for their children and their friends, where they can exchange addresses. Some children enjoy making scrapbooks of pictures and mementos. *Goodbye House*, by Nancy Evans and Ann Banks, is a write-in book for children about to move, in which they can paste photographs and record memories in answer to questions. Older children may need reassurance that they can still call their old friends sometimes after they move.

Children and parents should openly share their worries about moving. One mother returned from her first PTA meeting at a new school and admitted to her children, ''I used to like these meetings because I'd always see people I knew. But this was awful; I didn't have anyone to talk to.'' ''See?'' her nine-year-old daughter said, ''Now you know how we feel.''

If children are worried that they won't make friends, parents might want to talk with them about what to say to someone new. They could even role-play some situations. More reassuring, perhaps, is reminding them of their successes at making friends in the past: at camp, religious school, or on a vacation.

It takes time for families to develop roots in a new community, but the sooner they begin the better it is for everyone. Parents should encourage their children to join activities in which they will meet other children, to invite classmates home, and to take part in school and neighborhood events. If the move is made during the summer, for example, parents might take their children to the community swimming pool or park where other children play. They might explore the neighborhood together to find the best places to shop. If the move is made during the school year, parents can enroll their children in popular after-school activities. Parents should also lead the way by becoming involved in the community themselves. Any connections they make will ease the way for the whole family.

Handled well, the experience of moving can be a challenge that builds children's confidence and broadens their horizons. One father likes to tell the story of his son, whom he had carried screaming into a new school for the first day of third grade. "At the beginning of sixth grade," he concludes, "he was elected president of the student body."

But what about maintaining contact with the friends and family left behind? In *Helping Ourselves: Families and the Human Network*, Mary C. Howell, M.D., compares relationships to "muscle tissue, or a complex skill like piano playing. Used frequently, they grow in strength, stamina, intricacy, and the potential for enjoyment. Unused, they remain small or seem unfamiliar and foreign." Moving a great distance away is a direct threat to relationships. Sociologists Andrew J. Cherlin, Ph.D., and Frank F. Furstenberg, Jr., Ph.D., report in *The New American Grandparent* that adults feel compelled to keep in close touch with parents who live nearby and their children see them often. But when they move away, contact is much less frequent and the bond between grandparent and grandchildren is weakened.

Determined families who value these special relationships, however, find ways to sustain them. One woman got into the habit as a child of being a faithful correspondent. "My mother always wrote letters," she remembers. "I can still see her late at night writing away at the dining room table." Other families telephone friends and relatives regularly or send photographs or audio- or videotapes back and forth showing their activities. One family sends extra-large group postcards to grandparents, uncles, aunts, and cousins from wherever they visit. "This makes the kids think about these people whom they don't often see and tells them whom we consider part of our close family. I always say things like, 'Uncle Ben is a fisherman, so be sure to write about the fish you caught' or 'Grandma loves dogs; let's send her this card with the two puppies.' " Some families compile and save family scrapbooks and photo albums, keeping them up-to-date, so that children remain familiar with and somewhat involved with relatives they rarely see.

Preserving unique traditions also connects families with relatives distant in time as well as space. In one family the recipe for a seven-layer torte (translated from Serbo-Croatian) crossed the ocean and has now passed into the third generation. Its presence on special occasions always elicits stories, such as that of the grandfather who as a child demanded a whole torte of his own each year on his birthday.

Some families and friends reunite once or twice a year to celebrate birthdays or holidays, or they spend vacations together, building happy memories that can be relished for the next six months or year or even longer. A brother and sister, for instance, who fondly recall childhood beach vacations with their cousins, have tried to reproduce these with their own families. They feared that otherwise their children might grow up knowing their own cousins only as pictures on Christmas cards. They are building a common history together from memories of collecting shells and sharing sandy peanut butter sandwiches.

Some ambitious families plan mass reunions with relatives and/or friends, or both. For these events to succeed, advance planning is essential. Sometimes representatives chosen from each family group work together on the planning. The site is selected based on convenience and affordability for everyone. Some groups gather at a home or a park, or rent space at a hotel or resort. Others, who want more time together, might go camping together for a weekend. Food and activities should be organized well in advance, taking into consideration the ages of those attending. A family historian may be appointed to gather information for a family tree or a narrative of memories to be presented or shared at the next reunion.

Extended Families

''Large family, quick help'' is a Serbian proverb. It refers to the traditional extended family in which aunts, uncles, cousins, grown siblings, and grandparents lived near each other and provided love, joy, comfort, knowledge, skill, and support in times of crisis or need. They shared responsibilities and felt they could ask each other for help without embarrassment. In the past and in other societies, extended families also regularly cared for the young, the sick, and the elderly, and provided a complete and satisfying social circle. Many American families today, even those who live near relatives, could benefit from exploiting this resource more fully.

In her essay ''Interdependence,'' in *Family Strengths 4*, edited by Nick Stinnett et al., Carolyn Attneave, Ph.D., professor of psychology at the University of Washington, described a visit to the South Pacific, where she regularly encountered children being raised by an aunt or grandmother while their parents were at school, sick, or away for some other reason. She writes that this type of arrangement would be a problem or a trauma in mainstream American families, who have stripped themselves down to the nuclear family and, in some cases, a few relatives. In Fiji and Samoa, however, the normal family unit comprises 15 to 20 people. From the time children are born they are cared for by all the uncles, aunts, and other adults in this group. "Of course there is a sense of missing a mother or father who may have to be away for a while," Dr. Attneave writes, "but there is also a security that comes from having many other parental figures who nurture."

In America, the extended family traditionally has been strongest among the working class, blacks, and certain ethnic groups. In some cases, the stringent conditions of life—acquiring the basic needs of food, work, housing, and child care—may have united these families in order to pool resources. New Korean immigrants to the United States, for instance, often learn a trade, such as running a grocery, from other Koreans. Many then borrow money from family or friends to start their own businesses and employ family members, who work without pay.

Family members may also have been brought up to value one another's company. In *Growing Up and Growing Old in Italian-American Families,* Colleen Leahy Johnson, Ph.D., describes the important role the extended family plays in the daily life of Italian-Americans. "Relatives are often the focal point for sociability," she writes, "the source of much assistance, and in some cases facilitators to improve the financial standing of the nuclear family. . . . Rarely a week goes by that relatives do not play a central part in the average family's activities."

Some sociologists have pointed out, however, that strong kinship bonds do not come without a price. Although they can soften the bite of poverty or loneliness, they also can restrict the success of individual family members. Obligations to the group may deplete a family's savings, for instance, or prevent one member from pursuing a more lucrative job because it would mean moving too far away.

In recent years, as middle class wives and mothers have entered the work force and all families have experienced high rates of divorce, the extended family has been revived in the middle class as a source of support and a relief from stress. A working couple may need help caring for young children; a newly single mother may need temporary housing, child care, or financial help. Often the family members to whom parents turn first are grandparents.

Grandparents

Grandparents were rarely the standard fixtures in the families of the past that they have been in romanticized accounts. In fact, modern medicine and health care have made it possible for most of today's children to know most of their grandparents for the first time. While only 37 percent of the men and 42 percent of the women born in 1870 lived to the age of 65, 63 percent of men and 77 percent of women born in 1930 will live that long. Modern grandparents who do not live near their grandchildren are also able to communicate and travel long distances more easily than in the past. They generally have more leisure time, better health, and more money. Because of lower birth rates, they also have fewer grandchildren on whom to lavish these assets.

The relationship of grandparents to grandchildren in America has also changed in this century. As the generations have become more economically independent, the emotional ties among family members have become more important. According to Cherlin and Furstenberg in *The New American Grandparent*, many grandparents today feel that they have a closer and friendlier relationship with their grandchildren than their own grandparents did. In the past the relationship was based on respect. Today it is based more on affection and companionship. Though they have less direct authority over their grandchildren, the grandparents studied were happy with the emotional rewards of their roles. According to Arthur Kornhaber, M.D., in *Between Parents and Grandparents*, grandchildren are happy, too: "Not only were children with close grandparents more rooted in their families and communities, they felt very emotionally secure. . . . They had many people who were crazy about them."

Without an economic tie to their grandchildren, however, or the honorary role that some societies, such as in Japan, confer on their elders, American grandparents today have to extend themselves to create and sustain a meaningful relationship. Often they invest the most time and energy when children are young, establishing their claim through baby-sitting and other direct help.

In some families, however, this relationship fails and contacts with grandchildren are infrequent and strained. Some parents and grandparents do not get along well. Some parents feel that the grandparents are interfering too much, trying to tell them how to raise their children. Some complain that the grandparents compete with each other or with the parents for their grandchildren's affection and end up confusing and spoiling the children. Other parents, however, feel abandoned by grandparents who have moved to retirement areas and show little interest in seeing their grandchildren.

Some grandparents and parents have to work out anew their roles after divorce. Sadly, while the custodial grandparents tend to become more involved with the grandchildren, the noncustodial grandparents often are cut off from them. In families blended through a second marriage, grandparents may create unhappiness by showing too much favoritism toward their biological grandchildren.

Those who suffer most in families that have a strained or weak connection between generations are the children. They lose access to a part of their family heritage and miss the security of having the largest possible network of caring family members. Dr. Kornhaber urges families to try to resolve the problems that separate generations. If they cannot do this alone, he recommends getting help from a member of the clergy or a mental health professional.

For the whole family, a good relationship with grandparents can be a safety net in times of crisis. In families where there is a divorce, illness, death, or other setbacks, grandparents are often asked to step in and help. And as they grow older, grandparents themselves may need understanding and support from their children and grandchildren.

When the problems between parents and grandparents cannot be resolved, or the grandparents live too far away or have died, some families who desire intergenerational contact find unrelated older people to fill the gap. ''I enjoyed my grandmother very much and identified strongly with her independence and outspokenness,'' said a single mother. ''My own mother died several years ago, long before my daughter was born. So I have unofficially 'adopted' a grandmother in my neighborhood, a woman I have known for many years who rarely sees her own grandchildren. I'm sure we have enjoyed our arrangement as much as we would if we were actually related. It makes no difference to my daughter. She has her 'Grandma.' '' Some community or religious organizations, such as Project Dorot in New York City, encourage young people and families to become "friendly visitors" to lonely elders, pointing out that the benefits are mutual.

Nonfamily Networks

In *Helping Ourselves*, Dr. Howell describes two kinds of families, open and closed. Closed families satisfy all their needs with their own internal resources or with the help of outside professional agencies. Open families adjust their boundaries to include others whom they trust and care about for the purpose of mutual support. These others include all kinds of nonbiologically related people: honorary relatives ("Aunt" Rosie, for instance, who is Mom's best friend from college), other friends, colleagues, and neighbors. Often these are people with whom the parents have spent as much or more time and shared as many experiences as they have with family members.

Families form nonfamily networks for many reasons. Relatives may live too far away to see regularly or they may be estranged. "I have five women friends with whom I am especially close," said a mother. "We have known each other for years. They're more my sisters than are my own sisters, who live far from me and are much older than I am. We have shared everything and helped each other through weddings, childbirth, moving, problems with children and elderly parents. If I have a problem, I'm more likely to call one of them long before I would consider talking to one of my relatives."

Sometimes families find themselves linking up because of common interests. Neighbors often unite over a problem—a fight with a landlord or with the city over services, for instance. Parents who find themselves on the same side of a school issue may form friendships that continue long after the issue is resolved. Sometimes the common ground is a happier circumstance: raising money to improve a local playground or starting a Little League team. In Evanston, Illinois, a group of neighbors known as the "Deckbusters" volunteers to help families add decks to their houses.

Honorary family networks can spring up anywhere. Employer-sponsored working-parent seminars have spawned continuing groups. Across the country, many of the parenting programs, which offer child care and educational workshops, also sponsor mothers' or fathers' support groups that may develop lives of their own. At one church, for example, the members of a mothers' group that had rallied behind a member who had cancer, became so close that they continued to meet regularly for years (later including spouses) to discuss many life issues. In their book *Mixed Blessings*, Paul and Rachel Cowan decribe how members of their workshops for interfaith couples continued to meet once the scheduled sessions were over. Sometimes they discussed their problems or celebrated holidays together. "Sometimes," the Cowans write, "they forgot about religion and just went out to the movies or shared a Chinese meal. They continued to give each other emotional support even though each of the couples found a different resolution to their problems."

Parents often discover that their children's play groups are one of the richest sources of lifelong friendships, not only for their children but also for themselves. These groups usually consist of a small number of preschoolers who play together at regularly scheduled times with one or two parents supervising. Play groups give children the chance to develop relationships with other children and with caring adults and give parents the relief of sharing some of the burden of parenting. One set of play-group mothers arranged to meet for dinner several times a year at a restaurant, supposedly to discuss the children and work out kinks in the schedule. But they enjoyed each other's company so much that they kept up the dinners long after the children had started school and the play group had disbanded. The friendships eventually expanded to include husbands and the children's siblings.

Religious Networks

Many commentators believe that religion is less central to the lives of American families today than it was in the past. In recent years, many established Protestant denominations have experienced slower growth or even a loss of membership. Both Roman Catholics and Jews have married partners from other faiths in increasing numbers. The rate of such marriages for Catholics is about 40 percent, compared with about 18 percent in the 1920s. For Jews, the rate was only about 5 percent before 1960. It is now between 30 and 40 percent. (In contrast, 70 percent of Protestants marry out of their denomination, but only 18 percent marry non-Protestants.)

Some blame the apparent decline of religion on the modern reliance on science and technology for answers to life's questions. Others point to the difficulty some people have reconciling traditional church dogma with the problems of modern life. For some families, church attendance simply loses out in competition with other activities for limited family time.

Religion, however, is clearly not dead. According to the Princeton Religious Research Center, figures from a 1988 Gallup survey indicated that 65 percent of the total population of the United States belonged to a religious institution and 42 percent had attended services within the last week. When asked to rank the importance of religion in their lives, however, only 53 percent of respondents said it was "very important," compared with 75 percent in 1952, the first year of the survey.

At the same time, paradoxically, there has been a rapid rise of fundamentalism in all major religions: Protestantism, Catholicism, Judaism, and Islam. Some observers believe that this reflects the same periodic swing toward conservative values that has appeared recently in both politics and education. For others it is a sign that people have discovered the limits of science and the intellect. In *Who Needs God*, Rabbi Harold Kushner suggests that "people are looking for religious seriousness and are not finding it in the churches and synagogues, which have rooted themselves in a philosophy of accommodation to the world around them. . . ." Along with many other mainstream religious leaders, he worries that "some of [the appeal of fundamentalism] is a fear of freedom, a fear of making choices."

Historically, religion has served social needs as well as spiritual ones. It has created a community of fellowship and support for people with similar values. A Catholic mother quoted by journalist Evelyn Kaye in *Cross-Currents* said: "It's not even the religiosity or the ritual which I wish [my children] could have; it's not anything as heavy as that. It is much more a strong community involvement that I wish for them. You drift so much during the teenage years, and some kind of organized community involvement would give them an anchor."

Some people have looked outside existing religious institutions in order to adapt religion to their own needs and to find a satisfying combination of spirituality and community. In the Jewish Havurah movement, for instance, which began in the late 1960s, small groups of people meet to study, pray, and celebrate together. Whether or not they also join a synagogue depends on the desires of the individual members.

"Spiritual wellness," however families achieve it, is one of the major characteristics of strong families, according to Nick Stinnett, Ph.D., and John DeFrain, who in their book, *Secrets of Strong Families*, based on surveys of more than 3,000 families for the National Center for Family Strengths at the University of Nebraska. They describe this quality as sharing a belief in a higher power or greater good, which gives the family a sense of purpose and strength. This does not, however, require adherence to an organized religion. Living by a moral code, working for worthy causes, and caring for others all promote spiritual wellness.

Strength Within Families

As powerful and reassuring as the networks of family, friends, and social and religious communities are, they have the best chance to grow from families with a strong inner core. For parents, creating that core has always been a primary goal. Today, according to Dr. Bruno Bettelheim in *A Good Enough Parent*, this is best done through building strong emotional ties: "We must spend as much time and effort on [forging emotional ties] as parents in previous times spent working together with their children to keep the family going economically. . . . When the family managed to make a go of life, this made each of its members happy to belong to his family and gave him security. Today it is the emotional ties which must do all this. The stronger we make these ties, the more likely will our children grow into strong and secure persons."

Dr. Nick Stinnett and John DeFrain identified five specific

qualities, in addition to spiritual wellness, that contributed to the strength and happiness of the families they surveyed. All of these qualities relate to a family's emotional life:

- A commitment to each other's welfare and happiness
- Appreciation of each other
- Communication
- Spending time together
- The ability to cope with stress and crisis

Although this list is easy for most parents to accept, it is less easy to achieve these qualities in daily life. The best-intentioned family members can spend months passing each other in rooms, on the stairs, and at the table without any meaningful conversation. Piano lessons, soccer games, and parents' demanding jobs may keep everyone breathless and moving in different directions. Even when family members are all in the same room at the same time, telephones and television insidiously encroach on family life. According to a 1981 survey done by the Institute for Social Research of the University of Michigan, about one-fourth of the time that parents and children are together is spent watching television. A parent and child sitting side by side watching a TV sitcom are not likely to exchange many more words than if they were in different rooms.

In *Getting Closer*, Ellen Rosenberg recommends family meetings as a way to set aside time to be together and to ensure that everyone talks and listens to each other regularly. In a family meeting, anyone can raise a topic for discussion, state a problem or complaint, and share feelings. To start the process, Rosenberg suggests instituting a sharing box, in which family members can drop notes beforehand about what they want to bring up at the meeting. Parents may need to prompt younger children with questions such as "Did anything make you sad this week?" and "Did anything make you happy?" She believes that over time these meetings build trust and closeness in any family. They can be invaluable, however, for single parents, who need increased communication and cooperation to keep their families functioning.

Some families do not feel comfortable with anything quite so formal. They incorporate their communication and shared time into everyday activities. Reading together, biking together, and even doing chores can strengthen a family bond. One mother described the weekends her family spends at a cabin in the country. "It's time we spend as a family in a much less stressful environment," she says. "Even the children have put a certain amount of effort into making the place an acceptable home for us. They may help when we rake leaves or plant flowers. I think that kind of mutual effort of trying to improve something such as your home is very important to building family ties." Another mother talked about the regular weekly cleanup she does with her children. "We all pitch in and get the housework done in one morning. Everyone has assigned jobs, although we switch sometimes if someone wants to do something else. We play the radio so we'll have some motivation. Sometimes one of my children grumbles about these chores. But no one has missed a week yet. I know they take greater pride in their home because of it."

A sense of family history also strengthens the identity of a family. Taking pictures and mounting them in albums is one way to record family history. One family tape-records and transcribes everyone's memories of vacations so that they will have stories—in words as well as pictures—through which to relive them. One woman made copies of all the old family photos for her siblings, and each one set aside a wall for displaying them. Now whenever one family visits another, the children enjoy seeing the same pictures of their great-great-grandparents that they have in their own home.

Some parents take their children to visit the places where they grew up to give them a sense of their roots. This may be a little town in Greece or a neighborhood three blocks away. In either case, these sights add flesh to the stories about "When I was your age . . ." In Hawaii, the tradition of getting together to share family tales, called "talking story," is a common social activity.

Creating and maintaining family traditions reinforce the sense of family identity. These can be national, ethnic, or religious traditions—consisting of special handed-down holiday food and drink recipes; songs; or activities—or just-invented ones. One mother described a ceramic turkey that became a family tradition. "After we were grown," she says, "Thanksgiving was the one holiday when brothers and sisters all managed to make it to Mom and Dad's house with their families for dinner. Mom always put the cranberry sauce in a little ceramic turkey. But over the years, the turkey became chipped, and one year, it wasn't on the table. No one would sit down until that turkey was found, even though Mom insisted that it looked terrible. That year my sister took the turkey because she was afraid Mom would try to throw it out."

For children, these traditions also give order to the world, preparing them for what to expect. And for them, anything that happens twice is a tradition. Every time some children visit their grandfather, for instance, they work together on a 500-piece puzzle. The pile of finished puzzles is a concrete and satisfying reminder of the many weekends they have spent together.

Birthday and holiday celebrations are particularly compelling traditions for children. The sun barely sets on one birthday party before young children begin planning their next one and calculating how long (in twelfths of a year, if necessary) it will be before that special day arrives. Of these occasions, Dr. Bruno Bettelheim wrote, "Children stand in the center of affectionate attention and are made to feel important; the gifts they receive prove to them that they are loved and also that they are worthwhile people. If such occasions are celebrated in the right spirit, the glow from these days can spread out over the rest of life."

For small families, traditional times can be the occasions for regular gatherings of friends. A single mother described a yearly "surprise party" she and her friends have held for many years. "We would draw names at one party, then plan a little surprise gift for that person for the next party. As each of us married and had children, we included them in the surprise. We're now going into our twelfth year and no one would even think of not having the party, no matter how hard it is for some of us to get there."

And what is the result of all these elements combined? What is a strong family? One of the best descriptions comes from a 10-year-old girl quoted in *Episcopal Life* (May 1990) who was asked what her family meant to her: "The best thing about my family," she answered, "is the familiness. It's hard to explain the feeling of familiness. You know it when you feel it. It sort of has to do with being used to each other. I guess it is sort of to do with love."

Conclusion:
Raising Future Families

• • • • • •

Social scientists who have gazed into their crystal balls to read the future of the American family predict no surprises. "Were we to be transported suddenly to the year 2000," wrote Drs. Andrew J. Cherlin and Frank F. Furstenberg, Jr., in *The Futurist* magazine (June 1983), "the families we would see would look very recognizable. There would be few unfamiliar forms—not many communes or group marriages, and probably not a large proportion of lifelong singles. Instead, families by and large would continue to center around the bonds between husbands and wives and between parents and children." What change there is will be in the balance among existing family forms. In the year 2000 there probably will be even more single-parent families and families of remarriage than there are today and more two-wage-earner families.

Over the ages families have adapted successfully to much more dramatic upheavals. In America's development from an agrarian to an industrial society, the economic bonds that tied families together largely disappeared, to be replaced by the emotional bonds that still hold today. Relationships between husbands and wives, parents and children, and grandparents and grandchildren were all affected. Romantic expectations of marriage began to override those of financial support; children began to be valued for the psychological pleasure they brought their parents more than for their material contribution to the family enterprise; and grandparents became loving companions to their grandchildren rather than austere authority figures at the top of the family hierarchy.

Compared with this major social transformation, the changes that the present generation of parents and their children have had to weather may seem small: the increase in divorce and remarriage, the growing number of working mothers, the shortage of good child care, and the greater encroachment of the world's problems on family lives. Yet every day these men and women must decide how to behave in situations their parents never faced. They must create the models of mothers and fathers that their children will carry with them into adulthood and parenthood. And that responsibility is not at all small.

What are the issues that this generation of children will face as parents? Certainly the crying need for adequate child care for even the youngest children can only grow. Moreover, the next generation of parents probably will have to continue to press government at all levels, as well as businesses and schools, to create policies that recognize and benefit the many families of single parents, stepparents, and two wage earners.

The distribution of work in the household will also continue to be a family concern. Men may have to shoulder a fairer share, and children also may be called into service. According to sociologist Viviana A. Zelizer, Ph.D., in *Pricing the Priceless Child*, reviving the concept of the useful child, which reflects America's agrarian past, may benefit children as well as their families. The concrete, material contributions children can make to their family's welfare may give them more confidence in their personal worth than any vague psychological contribution does. ''The world of children is changing,'' Dr. Zelizer writes, ''and their household responsibilities may be redefined by changing family structures and new egalitarian ideologies. The notion, inherited from the early part of this century, that there is a negative correlation between the emotional and utilitarian value of children is being revised. The sentimental value of children may now include a new appreciation of their instrumental worth." She warns, however, that children would need to be protected from exploitation and that even a reorganized and more cooperative family unit could not nearly satisfy the vast needs of families today.

One new issue that today's children will have to confront, for which few of their parents will have prepared them, is the aging of American society. Whereas adults are living longer, the birth rate in recent years has tended to be lower. In the twenty-first century, however, for the first time in this nation's history, there will be more people over the age of 55 than people 14 and younger. As adults, more of today's children will bear the heavy emotional and practical burdens of caring for their elderly parents. According to Burton Reifler, M.D., of the Bowman Gray School of Medicine, "By the early 21st century adult day care will be just as accepted as day care for children is now" (Newsweek, July 2, 1990). It also will most likely have some of the same problems and inadequacies.

How can parents prepare their children for this and other unforeseeable issues in what undoubtedly will be a more complex world? The answer is simple: by doing what most parents already do. They try to satisfy children's basic needs for love, security, continuity, communication, identity, and belonging. And they try to apply good judgment, well-thought-out values, and an understanding of child development to all their child-rearing decisions. There is no better possible model of parenthood for whatever future lies ahead.

Resources

• • • • • •

Organizations

Alcoholics Anonymous (AA), P.O. Box 459, Grand Central Station, New York, NY 10163   (212) 686-1100
AA has chapters throughout the United States. Through AA meetings, men and women share their experiences to help themselves and others recover from alcoholism. It is self-supported through member contributions.

American Council on Alcoholism (ACA), 5024 Campbell Boulevard, Suite H, Baltimore, MD 21236   (301) 529-9200
The Council is concerned with promoting a national effort to educate youth about alcohol. Publications include the *ACA Journal*, *Research Quarterly*, and pamphlets. Literature on alcohol abuse and alcoholism is available to ACA members. Services to members also include a toll-free referral service.

American Council for Drug Education (ACDE), 204 Monroe Street, Rockville, MD 20850   (301) 294-0600
This nonprofit organization is dedicated to educating the nation about the health hazards of drugs. It believes that education is the first step toward preventing drug use and actively opposes the legalization or decriminalization of drugs. ACDE assists educators in their efforts to address drug use and provides background information to the media. It also publishes books, brochures, kits, pamphlets, and films to educate the public.

Association for the Care of Children's Health (ACCH), 3615 Washington Avenue N.W., Washington, DC 20016   (202) 244-1801
This organization of health-care workers, educators, and par-

ents is devoted to improving the ways in which professionals in health care respond to the unique emotional and developmental needs of children. It is committed to humanizing medical care for children and their families. ACCH publishes books and films for adults and children.

Child Care Action Campaign (CCAC), 330 Seventh Avenue, 18th Floor, New York, NY 10001   (212) 239-0138
The goal of this organization is to establish a national system of quality, affordable child care. It publishes information guides summarizing important family issues.

Institute for American Values (IAV), 250 West 57th Street, Suite 2415, New York, NY 10107   (212) 246-3942
The Institute is a nonprofit, nonpartisan organization concerned with issues affecting the American family. Its principal purpose is to deliver timely and useful research on family issues to the media. It seeks to bring family concerns into the mainstream of national policy debate. A biannual publication, *Family Affairs,* is available.

Mothers at Home, P.O. Box 2208, Merrifield, VA 22116 (703) 352-2292
This is an organization that supports mothers who choose not to work outside the home. It is dedicated to correcting society's misconceptions about women who opt to devote their full time to parenting. It also publishes a monthly newsletter in which mothers at home communicate with one another.

Narcotics Anonymous (NA), P.O. Box 9999, Van Nuys, CA 91409 (818) 780-3951
NA provides support for recovering addicts throughout the world. Using the Alcoholics Anonymous model, members meet regularly as a part of the recovery and drug-free maintenance programs. NA publishes a monthly newsletter.

National Association of Child Care Resource and Referral Agencies (NACCRRA), 2116 Campus Drive S.E., Rochester, MN 55904   (507) 287-2020
The purpose of NACCRRA is to promote the development, support, and expansion of quality child-care resource and referral services. NACCRRA works with over 250 child-care resource and

referral agencies from every state and publishes a quarterly newsletter.

National Association for the Education of Young Children (NAEYC),
1834 Connecticut Avenue N.W., Washington, DC 20009   (202)
232-8777

This organization provides educational resources for adults
who are committed to improving the quality and availability of
services for children from birth through age eight. There are more
than 72,000 members and 400 local, state, and regional affiliate
groups. Publications include pamphlets and brochures, such as
"How to Choose a Good Early Childhood Program," and a journal for members, *Young Children*.

National Center for Missing and Exploited Children, 2101 Wilson
Boulevard, Suite 550, Arlington, VA 22201   (703) 235-3900

This organization was established to stop victimization and exploitation of children through public education. It assists parents
searching for missing children as well as law-enforcement agencies handling difficult cases involving missing children and child
sexual exploitation. It publishes many books and other literature
dealing with various topics of concern and operates a toll-free hot
line: (800) 843-5678.

National Council on Alcoholism and Drug Dependence (NCADD),
12 West 21st Street, New York, NY 10010   (212) 737-8122

This nationwide organization combats alcoholism, drug addiction, and related problems. Its primary missions are education,
prevention, and public policy advocacy. It offers prevention
programs for alcoholism and other drug addictions. NCADD spon-
sors National Awareness Month in April and National Alcohol-
Related Birth Defects Awareness Week, beginning on Mother's
Day each year. Its services also include a national, toll-free help-
referral line: (800) NCA-CALL.

Parents' Resource Institute for Drug Education, Inc. (PRIDE), The
Hurt Building, Suite 210, 50 Hurt Plaza, Atlanta, GA
30303   (404) 577-4500

PRIDE is dedicated to preventing drug and alcohol use by adolescents. It offers a range of programs and services to parents,
youth, community organizers, and educators. Services include
the PRIDE questionnaire for grades 6 to 12, which allows com-

munities to monitor drug abuse among their youth; a training workshop for parents; and a network linking parents to resources in any region of the nation. It also publishes a quarterly newsletter.

Parents Without Partners, Inc., International Office, 7910 Woodmont Avenue, Suite 1000, Bethesda, MD 20814   (800) 638-8078

This organization comprises local chapters for single parents with or without custody (due to divorce, death, adoption, or lack of marital history) that sponsor family activities, workshops, conferences, and local meetings to provide support and encouragement. The international headquarters has an extensive collection of books and pamphlets and publishes *The Single Parent* magazine.

Single Mothers by Choice, P.O. Box 1642, Gracie Square Station, New York, NY 10028   (212) 988-0993

For women who have chosen or are considering single motherhood, information and moral support are available through this organization. Members are also offered the option of participating in anonymous research projects. A newsletter is published quarterly.

Stepfamily Foundation, Inc., 333 West End Avenue, New York, NY 10023   (212) 877-3244

This organization helps the increasing number of people living with stepparents or stepchildren. It provides information, conducts seminars, and creates awareness of problems in step-relationships. It publishes a quarterly newsletter and operates a telephone counseling service for members.

TARGET, c/o National Federation of State High School Associations, 11724 Plaza Circle, P.O. Box 20626, Kansas City, MO 64195   (816) 464-5400

TARGET, a component of the National Federation of State High School Associations, is committed to helping America's youth cope with alcohol and other drugs. TARGET trains volunteers to develop programs and publishes educational books and videos on alcohol and drugs.

Books for Adults

Atlas, Stephen L. *The Official Parents Without Partners Sourcebook.* Philadelphia: Running Press, 1984.
This manual offers practical advice and personal experiences from single parents on a range of topics including finances, decision making, discipline, communication, custody issues, and special needs.

Balter, Lawrence, Ph.D., and Anita Shreve. *Dr. Balter's Child Sense: Understanding and Handling the Common Problems of Infancy and Early Childhood.* New York: Simon and Schuster, 1985.
Providing practical, commonsense and specific advice on child rearing, well-respected child psychologist Dr. Lawrence Balter discusses contemporary issues and attitudes about such topics as deciding on child care, watching television, playing doctor, talking to strangers, and helping children through a divorce.

Barun, Ken, and Philip Bashe. *When Saying No Isn't Enough: How to Keep the Children You Love Off Drugs: A Prevention And Intervention Guide for Parents of Preschoolers, Preteens, and Teens.* New York: Signet/New American Library, 1989.
This is comprehensive and practical advice by a father of four, himself a former drug user. The authors offer advice on how to establish parental credibility, teach children refusal techniques, and create a home environment to help children stay away from drugs.

Bernstein, Joanne E., and Masha Kabakow Rudman. *Books to Help Children Cope with Separation and Loss: An Annotated Bibliography,* Vol. 3. New York: Bowker Co., 1989.
This excellent essay on how books help children cope with a variety of life situations provides an extensive annotated list of titles and is well indexed and easy to use.

Bettelheim, Bruno, Ph.D. *A Good Enough Parent: A Book on Child Rearing.* New York: Alfred A. Knopf, 1987.
Not another "how-to" book; this is instead a dense, rich, reflective psychoanalytical work on the parent-child relationship by the late, preeminent child psychologist. Bettelheim advises par-

ents to resist the impulse to create the child they would like to have and instead to help the child fully develop into the person the child wishes to and can fruitfully become.

Brazelton, T. Berry, M.D. *Working and Caring.* Reading, Mass.: Addison-Wesley, 1985.
Here is sensible and comforting advice for the working parent from the well-known pediatrician and child development expert, who balances his empathy for the parent with his concern for the child's well-being.

Burns, Cherie. *Stepmotherhood: How to Survive Without Feeling Frustrated, Left Out, or Wicked.* New York: Harper & Row, 1986.
Stepmother Cherie Burns gives frank, insightful, and practical advice on stepmothering. She has interviewed stepmothers across the country and consulted with family counselors, covering such topics as ex-wives, visitation schedules, money, vacations, sex, guilt, discipline, and housework.

Cassell, Carol, Ph.D. *Straight from the Heart: How to Talk to Your Teenagers About Love and Sex.* New York: Simon & Schuster, 1987.
This contemporary approach to sexuality, based on questions that teens ask, offers realistic advice on how to help your teenager make responsible sexual choices without experiencing the hang-ups of the past.

Cherlin, Andrew J., Ph.D. *Marriage, Divorce, Remarriage.* Cambridge, Mass.: Harvard University Press, 1981.
Sociologist Cherlin presents an historical profile of American families and statistical changes in marriage, divorce, and remarriage rates. Dr. Cherlin also offers perspective on the reasons for these changes and explains differences among racial, economic, and ethnic groups.

Cherlin, Andrew J., Ph.D., and Frank F. Furstenberg, Jr., Ph.D. *The New American Grandparent: A Place in the Family, a Life Apart.* New York: Basic Books, 1986.
Two leading sociologists of the American family explore the dilemma of modern intergenerational relationships. Basing their conclusions on a representative nationwide study, the authors present an insightful look at grandparents and their place in the family.

Cowan, Paul, and Rachel Cowan. *Mixed Blessings: Marriages Between Jews and Christians*. New York: Doubleday, 1987.

Drawing on personal experience, history, literature, and hundreds of in-depth interviews, the Cowans explore the issues of interfaith marriages. This fascinating and insightful account has the added bonus of sound advice.

Crewdson, John. *By Silence Betrayed: The Sexual Abuse of Children in America*. Boston: Little, Brown & Co., 1988.

Pulitzer Prize–winning journalist Crewdson explores the complex and confusing world of child sexual abuse. In addition to providing an overview of the situation, he sheds light on some of the causes and examines policies for handling this national issue.

Curran, Dolores, Ph.D. *Traits of a Healthy Family: Fifteen Traits Commonly Found in Healthy Families by Those Who Work with Them*. New York: Harper & Row, 1983.

Based on questionnaires sent to 500 family professionals including teachers, clergy, pediatricians, social workers, and counselors, columnist-educator-author Curran looks at what makes a healthy family and how to build on these strengths.

Damon, William, Ph.D. *The Moral Child: Nurturing Children's Natural Moral Growth*. New York: Free Press/Macmillan, 1988.

A respected psychologist in the field of social development and a professor of education at Brown University, Damon has written a clear and concise summary of the current research on children's morality with useful implications for parents and educators.

Degler, Carl N. *At Odds: Women and the Family in America from the Revolution to the Present*. New York: Oxford University Press, 1980.

Pulitzer Prize–winner Degler places into historical perspective the question, How is a woman's right to equal opportunity reconciled with the demands of family, which (he maintains) still require the subordination of her individual interests to the welfare of her children and husband?

Demos, John. *Past, Present, and Personal: The Family and the Life Course in American History*. New York: Oxford University Press, 1986.

Fascinating history of the American family explores differences and similarities in family life, child-rearing practices, adolescence, middle age, the role of the father, and the relevance of the past to today's policy-making decisions.

Einstein, Elizabeth. *The Stepfamily: Living, Loving & Learning.* Boston: Shambhala Publications, 1985.

This book, written by a woman who is both a stepdaughter and a stepmother, provides information and advice on how to keep blended families together and realize their potential for happiness and fulfillment; a sensitive exploration of the difficulties to be faced and the ways to overcome them.

Einstein, Elizabeth, and Linda Albert. *Strengthening Your Stepfamily.* Circle Pines, Minn.: American Guidance Service, 1986.

This book provides practical advice, strategies, and guidelines on how to strengthen your stepfamily by building on the differences, recognizing the challenges, and understanding the problems and potentials.

Elder, Glen H., Jr., Ph.D. *Children of the Great Depression: Social Change in the Life Experience.* Chicago: University of Chicago Press, 1985.

A longitudinal study of 167 individuals born in 1920–21 and followed through the 1960s sheds light on the relationship between economic deprivation in childhood and the course of later adult life.

Elkind, David, Ph.D. *The Hurried Child: Growing Up Too Fast Too Soon.* Reading, Mass.: Addison-Wesley, 1981.

This important book presents a ground-breaking look at the pressures contemporary life places on young children and gives advice, insight, and hope for solving problems.

Elkind, David, Ph.D. *Miseducation: Preschoolers at Risk.* New York: Alfred A. Knopf, 1987.

Dr. Elkind discusses how early miseducation can cause permanent damage to a child's self-esteem and subsequent attitude toward learning. He warns against the pressures of trying to raise a "superkid."

Ephron, Delia. *Funny Sauce: Us, the Ex, the Ex's New Mate, the Mate's Ex, and the Kids.* New York: Viking Press, 1986.

The author of *How to Eat Like a Child* and *Teenage Romance* has turned her pen to the new American family. Hilarious, wise, comic, and insightful, Ms. Ephron shares stories about her husband and two stepchildren.

Flowers, John V., Jennifer Horsman, and Bernard Schwartz. *Raising Your Child to be a Sexually Healthy Adult.* Englewood Cliffs, N.J.: Prentice-Hall, 1982.
This book offers practical advice on how to raise children to be confident about their own sexuality and sensitive to the needs and rights of others.

Galinsky, Ellen, and Judy David, Ed.D. *The Preschool Years: Family Strategies That Work—From Experts and Parents.* New York: Times Books, 1988.
Based on actual questions that emerged from hundreds of seminars conducted by the authors, this comprehensive and useful guide combines the most current child development research with the practical advice of experts and parents of preschoolers.

Gordon, Sol, Ph.D., and Judith Gordon, M.S.W. *Raising a Child Conservatively in a Sexually Permissive World.* New York: Simon & Schuster, 1989.
Here is clear-minded, reassuring, and helpful advice by leading educators in the field on what, when, and how much to tell children and teens about sex in order to help them grow into responsible, self-possessed adults.

Grollman, Earl A., Rabbi, and Gerri L. Sweder. *The Working Parent Dilemma: How to Balance the Responsibilities of Children and Careers.* Boston: Beacon Press, 1988.
Based on a survey of 1,000 children nationwide, the authors offer insights into the effects on children of having both parents work outside the home. They offer practical advice on how to combine successful careers with happy home lives.

Harrison, Beppie. *The Shock of Motherhood: The Unexpected Challenge for the New Generation of Mothers.* New York: Charles Scribner's Sons, 1986.
Can mothers and fathers really share parenting responsibilities? Does sharing mean giving up authority? Is there such a thing

as working without guilt? A warm and encouraging look at the modern problems and joys of motherhood by a mother of four.

Hechinger, Grace. *How to Raise a Street-Smart Child: The Complete Parent's Guide to Safety on the Street and at Home.* New York: Facts on File Publications, 1984.

Based on information from professionals and parents, *Glamour* magazine education columnist Hechinger gives practical, concrete suggestions on what, when, and how to talk to children about safety issues, including sexual abuse, without creating undo anxieties.

Hochschild, Arlie, Ph.D., with Anne Machung. *The Second Shift: Working Parents and the Revolution at Home.* New York: Viking Press, 1989.

Hochschild studied 10 sets of two-career parents over an eight-year period. In the resulting book she looks behind the image of the modern woman who "has it all." She tells their stories and shares their struggles to find time and energy for jobs, children, and marriage. A seminal work of popular sociology, written with compassion.

Howell, Mary C., M.D. *Helping Ourselves: Families and the Human Network.* Boston: Beacon Press, 1975.

Howell believes that families could be strengthened by developing community networks and utilizing the information, skills, and services of experts in more "convenient" ways. She provides an overview of changes and choices in social policies, living styles, and institutions.

Johnson, Colleen Leahy, Ph.D. *Growing Up and Growing Old in Italian-American Families.* New Brunswick, N.J.: Rutgers University Press, 1985.

Johnson urges social planners to look at close-knit Italian-American families to find examples of people who have managed to ease the transition to old age by caring for their elderly. She examines the rituals, celebrations, and values of this American subculture as well as external influences, such as intermarriage and the economy, and notes changes in traditional patterns.

Kalter, Neil, Ph.D. *Growing Up With Divorce: Helping Your Child*

Avoid Immediate and Later Emotional Problems. New York: Free Press/Macmillan, 1989.

Presenting a clear, compassionate, developmental approach to protecting young children and adolescents from the emotional fallout of divorce, Dr. Kalter provides invaluable guidance that helps parents and children cope with the problems specific to their own situations.

Kaye, Evelyn. *Cross-Currents: Children, Families, and Religion.* New York: Clarkson N. Potter, 1980.

Based on interviews with hundreds of families and clergy, journalist Kaye looks at a diversity of child-rearing practices in interfaith marriages. She explores attitudes toward religion, sexuality, ethics, and familial bonds.

Keshet, Jamie K. *Love and Power in the Stepfamily: A Practical Guide.* New York: McGraw-Hill, 1986.

Advice and strategies are offered by a family therapist who specializes in working with blended families.

Kornhaber, Arthur, M.D. *Between Parents and Grandparents.* New York: St. Martin's Press, 1986.

Besides exploring the pleasures, problems, and conflicts involved in grandparenting, this leading clinical authority in the field discusses the importance of grandparents to the happiness of children in a practical and inspirational manner.

Kraizer, Sherryll Kerns. *The Safe Child Book.* New York: Delacorte, 1985.

This commonsense approach provides strategies, guidelines, and specific tips for protecting children from abduction and sexual abuse.

Kushner, Harold, Rabbi. *Who Needs God.* New York: Summit Books, 1989.

With warmth, clarity, and force, the author of *When Bad Things Happen to Good People* shows how religious commitment can renew, refresh, and replenish us, making a difference in our own lives and helping us to make a difference in the lives of others.

LaFarge, Phyllis. *The Strangelove Legacy: Children, Parents, and Teachers in the Nuclear Age.* New York: Harper and Row, 1987.

A report on how children of various ages feel about growing up with the threat of nuclear war and how to help them handle their fears and be hopeful about the future. Encourages discussion and activism.

Lansky, Vicki. *Vicki Lansky's Divorce Book for Parents: Helping Your Children Cope with Divorce and Its Aftermath.* New York: New American Library, 1989.

This practical and warmly supportive manual goes step-by-step through all the stages of separation and divorce. Lansky gives advice that is age-specific for children and explains what kind of reactions to expect, how to respond, and when to seek professional intervention.

MacEachern, Diane. *Save Our Earth: 750 Everyday Ways You Can Help Clean Up the Earth.* New York: Dell, 1990.

While not absolving government and industry of responsibility for creating a cleaner environment, MacEachern urges individuals to act to make their own lives better and the world a better place for all.

Miller, Jo Ann, and Susan Weissman. *The Parents' Guide to Day Care.* New York: Bantam Books, 1986.

A comprehensive and clear guide on how to select and evaluate day-care facilities, with an emphasis on health and safety. The book also gives practical advice on how to make day care a happy, safe, and problem-free experience for all. It includes tips such as how to help your child adjust to separation and how to lessen the "hurry up, let's go" hassles of the morning.

Planned Parenthood Federation of America, Inc. *How to Talk With Your Child About Sexuality: A Parents' Guide.* Garden City, N.Y.: Doubleday, 1986.

Practical, comprehensive, no-nonsense guide for helping parents deal intelligently and comfortably with their children's questions about sex and relationships.

Pogrebin, Letty Cottin. *Growing Up Free: Raising Your Child in the 80's.* New York: McGraw-Hill, 1980.

The author describes nonsexist child rearing that seeks to nourish the unique person in every child with warm, compassionate common sense that touches all aspects of a child's life.

Pruett, Kyle D., M.D. *The Nurturing Father: Journey Toward the Complete Man*. New York: Warner Books, 1987.

This renowned Yale child psychiatrist challenges assumptions about paternal nurturing. He discusses the capacity of men as child-care givers and the benefits to children of involved fathers. He shares studies of families where the father is the primary nurturer. Significant reading for mothers and fathers.

Rosenberg, Ellen. *Getting Closer: Discover and Understand Your Child's Secret Feelings About Growing Up*. New York: Berkley, 1985.

This book discusses what children want and need to know and how to talk to them, including topics such as physical growth and development, teasing, friendships and popularity, peer pressure, and sexual feelings.

Rosin, Mark Bruce. *Stepfathering: Stepfathers' Advice on Creating a New Family*. New York: Simon and Schuster, 1987.

Providing advice and encouragement for men by men, this book presents the headaches, heartaches, and joys of raising stepchildren, written from personal experience and in-depth interviews with more than 50 stepfathers.

Sanger, Sirgay, M.D., and John Kelly. *The Woman Who Works, the Parent Who Cares: A Revolutionary Program for Raising Your Child*. New York: Perennial Library/Harper and Row, 1988.

This book emphasizes the ''need to be permissive with children's feelings, yet strict about their behavior.'' Provides explicit, practical advice as well as overall philosophy promoting ways of improved communication with children.

Savage, Karen, and Patricia Adams. *The Good Stepmother: A Practical Guide*. New York: Crown, 1988.

Containing an anecdotal approach that helps stepparents identify with and learn from familiar situations, this book discusses such topics as money, sex, the ex-wife, and the stages that stepfamilies go through from courtship onward.

Scarr, Sandra, Ph.D. *Mother Care/Other Care*. New York: Basic Books, 1984.

A developmental psychologist and mother of four, Scarr combines scholarly acumen, personal experience, and practical advice in solving some of the problems of modern parents. Particularly helpful for working mothers considering child-care options.

Schaefer, Charles E., Ph.D. *How to Talk to Children About Really Important Things*. New York: Harper & Row, 1984.

Based on common sense, current research, and practical experience, this book by child psychologist Dr. Schaefer discusses everyday concerns and stressful major life events. He provides guidelines, strategies, and tips on how to talk with children and how to be an "askable" parent. While being reassuring, warm, and straightforward, Dr. Schaefer stresses the importance of listening to and acknowledging the child's viewpoint.

Schulman, Michael, Ph.D., and Eva Mekler. *Bringing Up a Moral Child: A New Approach for Teaching Your Child to be Kind, Just, and Responsible*. Reading, Mass.: Addison-Wesley, 1985.

Sound, research-based "how-to" manual that not only advises but also explains moral development and the growth of conscience.

Schwebel, Robert, Ph.D. *Saying No Is Not Enough: Raising Children Who Make Wise Decisions About Drugs and Alcohol*. New York: Newmarket Press, 1989.

Dr. Schwebel offers strategies that parents can use with even very young children in order to empower them to make their own life-protecting decisions about drugs. He emphasizes that learning to say no is a family affair, not just a teenage problem.

Siegel-Gorelick, Bryna, Ph.D. *The Working Parents' Guide to Child Care*. Boston: Little, Brown & Co., 1983.

Solid information on the various alternatives to child care and guidance on deciding which choice is best for your child. Reflects the latest research and offers practical advice on issues such as interviewing, contracts, child development, and attachment concerns.

Sontag, Susan. *AIDS and Its Metaphors*. New York: Farrar, Straus and Giroux, 1989.

In this passionate and powerful sequel to *Illness as Metaphor*, social critic Sontag seeks to dispel myths and prejudices that people have about AIDS.

Spock, Benjamin, M.D., and Michael B. Rothenberg, M.D. *Dr. Spock's Baby and Child Care,* rev. ed. New York: Pocket Books, 1985.

The classic child-rearing manual offers comprehensive, reliable information about the physical and emotional health of children.

Spock, Benjamin, M.D. *Raising Children in a Difficult Time,* rev. ed. New York: Pocket Books, 1985.

A reassuring, commonsense approach to help parents and children through the difficulties of living in the modern world, by the man who wrote the book on baby care.

Stinnett, Nick, Ph.D., and John DeFrain. *Secrets of Strong Families.* New York: Berkley Publishing Co., 1986.

Two noted professors of family studies have observed over 3,000 families in the United States and abroad to discover what makes family life rewarding. They emphasize six major qualities that strong families share, qualities that don't protect them from problems but do enable them to survive and surmount difficulties.

Wallerstein, Judith S., Ph.D., and Sandra Blakeslee. *Second Chances: Men, Women and Children a Decade After Divorce.* New York: Ticknor and Fields, 1990.

This comprehensive 10-year longitudinal study details the long-term emotional, economic, and psychological effects of divorce on adults and children. The stories of different families in the study bring the complexities and issues of divorce into focus with more power than can be rendered by mere statistics, as the researchers look at how divorce is reshaping the American family.

Wallerstein, Judith S., Ph.D, and Joan Berlin Kelly. *Surviving the Breakup: How Children and Parents Cope with Divorce.* New York: Basic Books, 1982.

This important study explores and documents the immediate and long-range effects of divorce on children. The findings strongly suggest the need to rethink the entire process and consider ways to minimize some of the harmful effects on children.

Weiss, Robert S., Ph.D. *Going It Alone: The Family Life and Social Situation of the Single Parent.* New York: Basic Books, 1981.

Sociologist Weiss discusses the life of the single parent. In their own words, single parents tell about the everyday problems of raising children, how they cope, and how they feel.

White, Burton L. *Educating the Infant and Toddler*. Lexington, Mass.: Lexington Books, 1987.
Reliable, practical information by the renowned researcher on what is and is not known about the learning process and developmental stages of young children; authoritative and readable.

Yogman, Michael W., and T. Berry Brazelton, M.D., eds. *In Support of Families*. Cambridge: Harvard University Press, 1986.
The authors examine the effects of current societal stresses on families and explore strategies for coping. The emphasis of the book is on policy implications, urging more supportive and enlightened government and corporate involvement.

Youcha, Geraldine, and Judith S. Seixas. *Drugs, Alcohol, and Your Children: How to Keep Your Family Substance-Free*. New York: Crown, 1989.
Common-sense guide to how children (from preadolescence to adulthood) become involved in drugs and how to help them recover. Includes warning signs, a drug dictionary, and useful sources of information and help.

Zelizer, Viviana A. *Pricing the Priceless Child: The Changing Social Value of Children*. New York: Basic Books, 1985.
Sociologist Zelizer traces the transformation in the economic and sentimental value of children between the 1870s and the 1930s, when the role of children changed from useful economic asset to priceless love object.

Books for Children

Andrews, Jan. *Very Last First Time*. Illustrated by Ian Wallace. New York: Atheneum, 1986.
An Inuit girl discovers a fantastic and beautiful world on the

ocean floor when she goes beneath the thick winter ice for "the very last first time." (Ages 4–7)

Anno, Mitsumasa. *Anno's Medieval World.* Adapted from the translation by Ursula Synge. New York: Philomel Books, 1980.
This elegantly crafted book presents an episode in the history of ideas for children. It challenges readers to think about how ideas take hold of a society and how they grow and change. It asks the reader to think about the human cost of these ideas and to appreciate the suffering of the people who struggled to give them life. (Ages 7 and up)

Anno, Mitsumasa. *Anno's U.S.A.* New York: Philomel Books, 1983.
Travel coast to coast, through past and present, through intricate scenes of rural and city life. This book is full of allusion and illusion to pore over again and again. (All ages)

Ashabranner, Brent. *Always to Remember: The Story of the Vietnam Veterans Memorial.* Photographs by Jennifer Ashabranner. New York: Dodd, Mead, 1988.
The story behind the Vietnam War Memorial: the man who conceived it, the woman who designed it, the controversies surrounding it, and the lost lives it honors. (Ages 11 and up)

Ashabranner, Brent, and Melissa Ashabranner. *Into a Strange Land.* New York: Putnam Publishing Group, 1987.
The plight of unaccompanied refugee children and their struggles to make a new home in the United States are explored in this moving and insightful book. (Ages 10–15)

Brown, Laurene Krasny, and Marc Brown. *Dinosaurs Divorce.* Boston: Little, Brown, 1986.
Direct, simple text and lively, humorous illustrations of dinosaur families make this a timely and reassuring resource for young children and their parents with positive suggestions for handling the new and difficult situations and feelings that divorce can bring. (Ages 7–9)

Browne, Anthony. *Piggybook.* New York: Alfred A. Knopf, 1986.
One day, overworked Mrs. Piggott walks out on her husband

and sons, declaring "You are pigs." Indeed they are, but when they learn to care for themselves, the family is reunited. Humorous illustrations abound with pigs. Try to find all of them! (Ages 4 and up)

Cleary, Beverly. *Dear Mr. Henshaw.* Illustrated by Paul O. Zelinsky. New York: William Morrow, 1983.

A lonely fourth grader, in letters to his favorite author, reveals how much he wishes his divorced parents would get back together, how much he misses his father, and the trials of school life. This 1983 Newbery Award–winner is funny, sad, and very real. (Ages 9–14)

Clifton, Lucille. *Everett Anderson's 1-2-3.* Illustrated by Ann Grifalconi. New York: Holt, Rinehart, and Winston, 1977.

When his mother starts seeing Mr. Perry, Everett starts thinking about numbers: One is lonely, two is just right, and three is too crowded. Mama's new happiness helps Everett to change his mind. (Ages 4–7)

Cohen, Barbara. *Molly's Pilgrim.* Illustrated by Michael J. Deraney. New York: Lothrop, Lee, & Shepard Books, 1983.

A class learns that not all the pilgrims to our country arrived in the 1620s. A touching story that makes clear the real meaning of Thanksgiving. (Ages 5–9)

Cole, Brock. *The Goats.* New York: Farrar, Straus and Giroux, 1987.

What begins as a cruel prank played on them by their fellow campers turns into an adventure in survival for Howie and Laura, as they learn about themselves and each other. This emotionally tense and thoroughly rewarding reading experience ponders the nature of justice and true intimacy between the sexes. (Ages 11 and up)

Dana, Barbara. *Necessary Parties.* New York: Harper Junior Books, 1986.

Dana tackles the complex issue of family responsibilities as she focuses on the impending divorce in the Mills family. Fifteen-year-old Chris feels his parents are acting irresponsibly and takes them to court. This is an insightful, wise, and often hilarious novel. (Ages 12 and up)

DePaola, Tomie. *Oliver Button Is a Sissy*. San Diego: Harcourt Brace, 1979.

Teased because he'd rather dance than play ball, Oliver eventually wins respect by dancing to his own tune. (Ages 4–8)

The Earth Works Group. *50 Simple Things Kids Can Do to Save the Earth*. Kansas City, Mo.: Andrews and McMeel, 1990.

Full of consciousness-raising facts about how people today carelessly damage the environment and easy experiments and activities kids can do at home to change that. (Ages 8–12.)

Evans, Nancy, and Ann Banks. *Good-bye House*. New York: Clarkson Potter, 1980.

A fill-in book with activities to preserve children's memories of their old home and acquaint them with their new one. Helpful introduction for parents. (Ages 8–12).

George, Jean. *Watersky*. New York: Harper Junior Books, 1982.

Adventure, romance, and the clash of cultures combine in this story about Lincoln, who goes to Alaska to search for his uncle and unearths secrets of the whales, the northland, and his own heart. (Ages 11–15)

Girard, Linda Walvoord. *My Body Is Private*. Illustrated by Rodney Pate. Niles, Ill.: A. Whitman, 1984.

This sensitive, sensible, and careful guide distinguishes between good and bad touching. It emphasizes children's rights to autonomy over their own bodies. (Ages 5–9)

Gordon, Sol, and Judith Gordon. *A Better Safe Than Sorry Book: A Family Guide for Sexual Assault Prevention*. Illustrated by Vivien Cohen. Ed-U Press, 1984.

The authors advise about what to do if children are abused, stress loving relationships between adults and children, and encourage children to demand respect for themselves. (Ages 3–8)

Hazen, Barbara Shook. *Tight Times*. Illustrated by Trina Schart Hyman. New York: Viking Press, 1979.

Dad's unemployment means tight times for the family. A conflict over a pet brings frustrations into the open and allows for the eventual strengthening of family bonds. (Ages 5–8)

Hest, Amy. *The Purple Coat*. Illustrated by Amy Schwartz. New York: Four Winds Press, 1986.

Each year Grandpa makes Gabrielle a new navy coat. This year she wants a purple one. Gentle humor and shared memories help them to reach a creative solution to this dilemma. (Ages 4–7)

Hyde, Margaret O., and Elizabeth H. Forsyth. *AIDS: What Does It Mean to You?* New York: Walker, 1987.

This skillfully done overview of the AIDS epidemic gives scientific facts in a compassionate, clear, and accessible way. (Ages 12 and up)

Jukes, Mavis. *Like Jake and Me.* Illustrated by Lloyd Bloom. New York: Alfred A. Knopf, 1984.

Jake and his new stepson, Alex, realize that they have a lot in common in a warm, humorous story of a loving family. (Ages 5–10)

Kleeberg, Irene Cumming. *Latchkey Kid.* Illustrated by Anne Canevari Green. New York: Franklin Watts, 1985.

This book provides much information and advice for kids who are often on their own. (Ages 9–13)

Lord, Bette Bao. *In the Year of the Boar and Jackie Robinson.* Illustrated by Marc Simont. New York: Harper and Row, 1984.

When "Bandit" Wong's family comes to Brooklyn from China, she chooses "Shirley Temple" as her American name. This family story of growing up in the 1940s has relevance for today. (Ages 8–10)

Mansfield, Sue, and Mary Bowen Hall. *Some Reasons for War: How Families, Myths and Warfare Are Connected.* New York: Crowell Junior Books, 1988.

This provocative and important book traces the history of war from the Stone Age to the Nuclear Age and offers theories on why warfare plagues humankind. (Ages 11 and up)

Paulsen, Gary. *Hatchet.* New York: Bradbury Press, 1987.

Thirteen-year-old Brian is the only survivor of a plane crash, and he must make it on his own in the wilderness with only a hatchet to aid him. This engrossing tale of physical endurance, emotional growth, and the gathering of inner resources is told with great authenticity. (Ages 10–15)

Polacco, Patricia. *Meteor!* New York: Dodd, Mead, 1987.

News travels, rumors fly, and stories grow after a meteor crashes into the Michigan farmyard of Grandma and Grandpa Gaw. Based on actual events, this exuberant picture book should inspire readers to exhume their own local and family stories. (Ages 5–10)

Pryor, Bonnie. *The House on Maple Street*. Illustrated by Beth Peck. New York: William Morrow, 1987.

By the time Chrissy and Jenny find an arrowhead in a tiny china teacup and begin to wonder how it found its way into their garden, we have already learned how their very house came into being. A fascinating look at 300 years of American history and an imagination grabber. (Ages 5–9)

Rosenberg, Maxine. *Being Adopted*. Photographs by George Ancona. New York: Lothrop, Lee & Shepard Books, 1984.

Children of various ethnic backgrounds share their feelings about their new families, illustrated with excellent black-and-white photographs. (Ages 9–14)

Seixas, Judith. *Drugs: What They Are, What They Do*. Illustrated by Tom Huffman. New York: Greenwillow Books, 1987.

This book is a well-handled explanation of various drugs and why kids take them. (Ages 7–10)

Seixas, Judith. *Living with a Parent Who Takes Drugs*. New York: Greenwillow Books, 1989.

Seixas gives realistic and honest advice along with coping strategies emphasizing how to get help in emergencies. Written with candor and compassion. (Ages 10–15)

Index

· · · · · ·

244